# Leading witl
## to Give

# 'The Undefended Leader' trilogy of books by Simon Walker

## Book 1: *Leading out of Who You Are*

Leadership involves power and influence over others—but each of us is trapped by a psychological imperative inside us to use whatever control we have for our own ends. Where does this imperative come from? From our sense of self, formed during our childhood, which is the source of our drives and fears. The author describes four ego patterns—Shaping, Defining, Adapting or Defending—and shows how they determine the needs we try to meet in our lives as leaders. Our natural instinct to use our leadership to meet our own needs rather than others' is what he terms 'defendedness'.

One strategy of defended leadership is to build a 'front stage' and a 'back stage', which allows us to reveal or conceal aspects of our self according to how threatening we perceive our audience to be. While the best human audiences (in secure relationships, loving marriages, deep friendships and so forth) can go some way towards fulfilling our need for unconditional and dependable approval, ultimately we need to locate a spiritual source of approval if we are to be fully available to serve others freely. Study questions and exercises, as well as leadership tools and an online community, help readers to discover ways to develop greater undefendedness.

## Book 2: *Leading with Nothing to Lose*

The journey to undefended leadership doesn't stop at a personal discovery. It should continue towards a new approach to the tasks of leadership. This book ventures into the territory of the pragmatic leader who has to make executive decisions, manage budgets, set targets, hire and fire, resolve conflict, improve performance, organize procedures, plan strategy...

The author illustrates from history eight different styles of exercising power (which he calls Foundational, Commanding, Affiliative, Serving, Pacesetting, Visionary, Consensual and Self-emptying), and explains why the ability to use not just one or two of these but all of them fluidly—and for the benefit of others, not ourselves—depends not simply on skill or training but (paradoxically) on the freedom to abandon our defences and attend to the needs of those around us. Indeed, as long as we are afraid of what we might lose, we remain unable to access the most radical and powerful of the leadership strategies: self-emptying. The Holy Grail of leadership—the ability to use each of the eight strategies as and when needed—is found only by those who, like Mahatma Gandhi or Martin Luther King, take the risk of 'leading with nothing to lose'.

## Book 3: *Leading with Everything to Give*

The personal character of the leader and the pragmatics of leadership lead us outwards towards the question we must now address: the politics of the leader. That is the focus of this last, and arguably most urgent, book in the trilogy.

# Leading with Everything to Give

## Lessons from the Success and Failure of Western Capitalism

### Book 3 of
### THE UNDEFENDED LEADER trilogy

### Simon Walker

PIQUANT
editions

# Contents

# Acknowledgements

I am grateful to the many people who have supported me over the last nine years as this book has taken shape. In particular, I have appreciated those many students who, during my courses, have given me valuable encouragement to take these ideas out to a wider audience.

I am grateful also to my publisher and my editor, Huw Spanner, who have stuck with this project from its embryonic form right through to its birth as a fully-formed trilogy.

Most of all, I am grateful to my children, Barnaby, Jonah and Olivia, whose patience towards a distracted father has, at times, been stretched beyond the acceptable. For them, and their generation, I have written this book in the hope that I and my generation will leave the world in a better state than we found it.

Simon Walker

# Preface

These are difficult days. The collapse of Lehman Brothers on 16 September 2008 marked the beginning of a period of economic collapse that, at the time of writing, is still unfolding day by day. My own business suffered the immediate effects of the crisis: clients promptly cancelled projects and deferred all non-essential investment, as they took measures to cut costs—including lay-offs and sell-offs—that are now becoming only more severe. None of us knows how deep, or prolonged, the downturn will prove to be, or quite what the world will look like when we emerge from it. Our financial models are simply not sophisticated enough to cope with the unprecedented complexity of these global events. The truth is that most of us today are scared.

At the same time, however, we should be absolutely clear that nothing that is now taking place is either surprising or unexpected. I wrote the first draft of this book more than two years ago, and the thinking it is based on was done well before that. I am not alone in the opinion that the factors that have caused this collapse were evident to anyone who had eyes to see them. The truth is that most of us, including our financial and political leaders, chose not to.

The broad thrust of this book is that Western civilization is nearing the end of its current life-cycle. If we locate its intellectual origins in the European Renaissance in the 15th century, we can trace from there a line of cultural development and flourishing that is now coming to an end. The industrial expansionism, the economic models of capital ownership, the organization of political power, the structure of our societies, all have lost their intellectual, practical and moral purchase. It is not that they are bankrupt in themselves but that our expression and application of them have become corrupt. The present economic crisis is merely a manifestation of a wider, more systemic breakdown in our civilization.

Thus, though it is economic turmoil that fills our foreground, we must not look for an answer that is purely economic. Our problems go far deeper. Our self-analysis must be more rigorous, more ruthless. It is incumbent on us, as the immediate dust settles, to ask how we got to this position, what impelled us to be so irresponsible and why our leaders failed to prevent it. Such questions insist that we explore our wider sociological, psychological and intellectual footings for an answer.

In fact, this is a time of great opportunity—of opportunity, in fact, on a scale not seen for several centuries perhaps. Over the next 50 years we have the chance to bring about a new Renaissance, with a new vision of what it means to be fully human. The glories of Venice, Florence, Sienna and other cradles of that cultural renewal in the 15th century remind us of our legacy in the West: architecture of extraordinary beauty and exquisite craftsmanship, art and music of sublime sensitivity. That period saw the birth of both modern science and modern literature, and the careful construction of a theology and philosophy robust enough to bear the weight of systems of governance that have brought forth arguably the greatest progress in political history.

Once again, we need a cultural rebirth, from which will grow a new social, economic and spiritual landscape. We must be aware, however, that such a rebirth cannot precede, let alone prevent, the demise of what has stood before. The shattered colossus of Shelley's Ozymandias reminds us of the inevitability of the death that must come first. We need courage to face our present loss, severe and painful as it is. We must take the first steps towards the future with a deep humility, aware that (as T S Eliot put it in 'Little Gidding') we come at night like a broken king, not knowing what we came for, in the hope that the purpose will break forth even as it is fulfilled.

Simon Walker
Oxford, 2008

# PART I

## DECONSTRUCTION:

## LESSONS FROM THE FAILURES OF WESTERN CAPITALISM

# ONE

## Laying Out the Map

In the first two books of this trilogy, I have used the model of the 'ecology' of power to illustrate the interactions of power and personality. Rather like a map, I have used it to set out the different regions (as it were) in which we might venture to exercise power, so that each of us can chart how and where we do so. It also helps us each to understand the impact of our actions on others (because if you choose to exert power in one region, it will also have an effect in another region). This 'ecology' functions as a whole: no one part of it can be separated out in isolation. The model shows us how we are interrelated, the character of the 'space' between one person and another.

This same idea will form the basis for our observations of society as a whole in this third and final book of the trilogy. We are interested in the interrelations not just between individuals but between whole populations. We are concerned to understand the flow of power between people(s). We want to know, if one population does this or that (spends its money in this way, for instance, or restricts freedom of speech in that way), what will happen to another population within the same social system. We want to understand how societies are connected as wholes, how they relate within themselves and between themselves. And to help us in this endeavour, I will be using a specific model of social ecology that I have developed over the past five years.

This particular model envisages three dimensions in which social interaction takes place.

### *Presented and reserved*
### *(also known as 'frontstage and backstage')*

'Presented' (or 'frontstage') and 'reserved' (or 'backstage') describe the two ways in which a social system can be perceived and experienced. On the one hand, a society has elements in it that are explicit for all to see—-which might include the image it chooses to project, the way it portrays itself, the 'visible landscape' of its culture, its overt industries, occupations and trades, its apparent rulers and authorities. All these are things that are 'presented' by that society to the wider world. They can be contrasted with those things that are 'reserved' by that society from such exposure—its underclass, most obviously, but also (for example) those values, beliefs, traditions and tales that express its history and character but are not always recited publicly. Every society has assumptions, attitudes, mores, taboos, ideas and stories that shape and inform it profoundly but are not apparent to the average tourist. You have to dig for them.

**Presented**
(What is visible)

**Reserved**
(What is hidden)

## Strong and weak

'Strong' and 'weak' differentiate the two kinds of power that groups in society exert over others. Strong power is a force that is directive, shaping or determining the response of others. Weak power is a force that is responsive, reacting to or following the action and direction of others. So, for example, *haute couture* fashion exerts strong power, setting a direction in design that the high street then follows. When scientists create a new drug that revolutionizes the treatment of cancer, they apply a strong force to medical practice as doctors change how they do things accordingly. If they don't comply, legal sanctions can be applied. On the other hand, if a man goes to the doctor about a lump or a bump in his body that is worrying his wife (however much, being a typical male, he might prefer to ignore it), she is exerting weak power over him. His love and respect for her oblige him to go, even though she has no (strong) power to compel him to.

**Strong power**
(What is directive)

**Weak power**
(What is responsive)

## Expanding and consolidating

'Expanding' and 'consolidating' refer to the two directions in which a force can move the society. An expanding force moves it on onto new ground, resulting in new ideals, new ideas, new aspirations, new enterprises. For example, immigration breaks up old social structures and exposes society to new cultures and new possibilities (as well as, potentially, new problems). On the other hand, a consolidating force establishes society on familiar ground. Conventions, traditions, institutions, governance and compliance with government are all examples of this. Families exert a cohesive force within a society, binding individuals into older, 'familiar' patterns of life, exerting discipline, nurturing emotional stability and health. So do strong local communities, voluntary organizations and schools.

Expanding drive
(Brings change)

Consolidating drive
(Brings stability)

Of course, these three 'dimensions' are not isolated from each other, but rather they interact with each other. In fact, they combine in eight different ways, which I denote by eight different three-letter 'codes'.

| | Strong/weak | Expanding/ consolidating | Legend |
|---|---|---|---|
| **Presented or frontstage** | Strong + | Consolidating | (PSC) |
| | Strong + | Expanding | (PSX) |
| | Weak + | Consolidating | (PWC) |
| | Weak + | Expanding | (PWX) |

| | Strong/weak | Expanding/ consolidating | Legend |
|---|---|---|---|
| **Reserved or backstage** | Strong + | Consolidating | (RSC) |
| | Strong + | Expanding | (RSX) |
| | Weak + | Consolidating | (RWC) |
| | Weak + | Expanding | (RWX) |

We could represent these eight different combinations as sectors on a map that represents a society. We would expect the character of each sector to be different and distinctive, as it expressed the particular dynamics of visibility, power and stability that governed that part of society. The diagram on page 6 illustrates what those distinctive characteristics might look like.

The model of social ecology gives us, as it were, a map with which we can make sense of our current political and economic landscape. Only when we can see our particular situation in the context of the whole will we be able to find the way ahead.

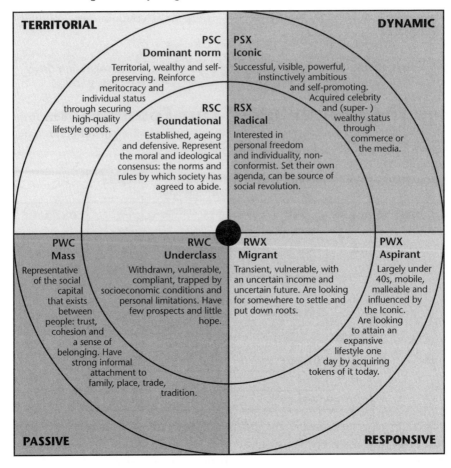

The model of social ecology applied to a society

# TWO

# The Crumbling of Our Foundations (RSC)

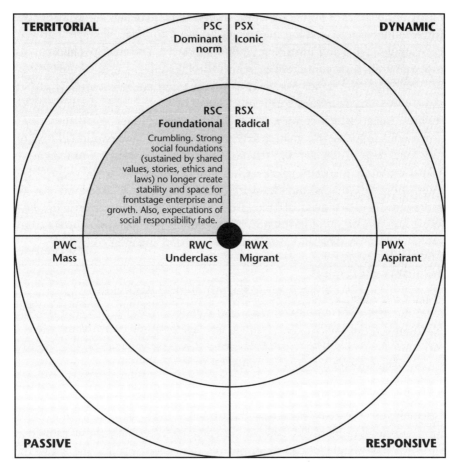

| TERRITORIAL | | | DYNAMIC |
|---|---|---|---|
| | **PSC**<br>Dominant<br>norm | PSX<br>Iconic | |
| | **RSC**<br>**Foundational**<br>Crumbling. Strong<br>social foundations<br>(sustained by shared<br>values, stories, ethics and<br>laws) no longer create<br>stability and space for<br>frontstage enterprise and<br>growth. Also, expectations of<br>social responsibility fade. | RSX<br>Radical | |
| PWC<br>Mass | RWC<br>Underclass | RWX<br>Migrant | PWX<br>Aspirant |
| **PASSIVE** | | | **RESPONSIVE** |

The current weakening of foundations in the West

## Chapter summary

In this chapter, we explore the Foundational aspect of Western society. The code for this sector is RSC, with each of these letters referring to a basic aspect of the social system.

The R stands for *'reserved'* (as opposed to P for 'presented'). Reserved elements of a society include its traditions, beliefs and values and the stories that express its history but may not always be told publicly. The S stands for *'strong force'* (as opposed to W for 'weak force'). Strong force is that which is directive and shapes or otherwise determines the response of others. The C stands for *'consolidating'* (as opposed to X for 'expanding'). Consolidating force anchors society to familiar ground—time-honoured habits, ways of relating, institutions, festivals, forms of governance and compliance. For example, families act as a cohesive force within society, keeping individuals bound into older, 'familiar' patterns, exerting discipline and nurturing emotionally stable and healthy children. So, too, do strong local communities, schools and voluntary organizations.

So, the code RSC stands for 'reserved, strong and consolidating'. Together, these three characteristics form an element of society which I have called 'Foundational': which is not easily visible ('reserved') but nonetheless exerts a powerful influence on that society's cultures, laws, behaviours and so on ('strong') so as to stabilize and strengthen that social system ('consolidating'). Like a building, a society needs such a foundation if it is to be secure. The foundation sets the boundaries within which acceptable freedoms can be expressed. It curbs individuals' impulses. It supplies a shared narrative in which individuals find meaning and identity. Undermining it renders the superstructure of that society unstable and at risk of disintegration and even collapse.

## Summary statement

*Western society has systematically undermined its own social, moral and economic foundations over the last century. The result is an inevitable fracture of its internal fabric, and an instability that threatens even more catastrophic collapse unless it is remedied as a matter of urgency. The ground beneath us has already shifted and we are witnessing the first signs of subsidence.*

................................................

Let's be clear: the economic crisis that exploded in the early autumn of 2008 was not caused primarily by bad banking practices. Certainly these resulted in an unbearable weight of bad debt, but the fundamental faults that led to the accumulation of that debt lie further back in the past, and are much less easy to see. The problem lay—indeed, still lies—with a crumbling of our social, moral and political disciplines that began about a century ago.

A few years back, my wife and I were house-hunting. One of the properties we viewed was a lovely old Victorian gabled house, now 'in need of some modernization' (as the real-estate agent's notes euphemistically put it). We could see at once that it needed total redecoration and some internal reordering, but some other, more fundamental problems soon became apparent. The wiring was 70 years old, the plumbing and boiler were archaic and there was no central-heating system at all. The infrastructure was looking dodgier all the time. And then we spotted the crack. Over a bay window on the side of the house that was built above a steeply sloping bank, a nasty-looking fissure had opened up. One look at that and we knew that if we bought the place we would be in for a whacking bill, simply to stabilize the building. Its foundations on the slope had sunk, and that entire side of the house had dropped.

The house had a fault line only one centimetre wide—not a lot, you might think. However, it pointed to bigger structural problems below the surface, problems that could threaten the entire building. Moreover, the cost to fix these problems would be immense. It's relatively cheap to lay deep and strong foundations when you put up a building, but to underpin an existing one that is sinking is an entirely different matter, requiring complex and expensive engineering work. It's always extremely difficult to reinforce foundations that are too shallow once the building has been erected on top.

## *Social foundations provide stability*

Human societies are not unlike buildings. Just as a building needs to have strong, deep, stable foundations hidden away underneath it, so the establishing of strong, consolidating patterns of power on the 'back stage' of a human social system is essential to give it stability. Thus, for example, the Roman Empire was built upon the training and organization of its legions. Without the agreements, sanctions, rewards and resources required to assemble and then manage a highly cohesive, disciplined army, the governance of that vast territory would have collapsed. Again, the British Empire was built upon the strict hierarchy shaped by the class system and the Christian religion. Respect for authority, dutiful obedience to God and Monarch and the Protestant work ethic were all crucial components in Britain's ascendancy from the 16th century onwards. Likewise, the extraordinary capacity of the Japanese to make tremendous sacrifices in the Second World War was the product of a highly ordered society in which devotion to the Emperor was paramount and surrender was a disgrace worse than death.

## *Social foundations allow freedom*

The foundations that support social systems and give them stability and resilience have to be laid down and reinforced consciously and deliberately. They do not come about by accident. The great freedoms set out by Thomas Jefferson in the American Declaration of Independence in 1776 laid down a philosophical and ideological foundation for the legal structure of the Constitution to be agreed in 1787. They represented fundamental shared beliefs about the nature of human life and civic responsibility: 'We hold these truths to be self-evident, that all men are created equal, that they are endowed by their Creator with certain unalienable Rights, that among these are Life, Liberty and the pursuit of Happiness.' On them was to be built the entire commercial and cultural civilization that developed over the following centuries. The Constitution is the American family's agreement on how things are going to be done, what is shared in common, what citizens are responsible for and what membership of the United States involves for each and every individual.

It is no coincidence that such fundamental principles should have been laid down at the beginning of the 13 states' new-won independence. Just as with a house, the foundations must come first before the walls and roofs can be constructed. Indeed, it is the strength and solidity of those foundations that will determine how stable the social structure will be that is built upon them, and how long it will last. Nation-building is much like any other form of building: problems arise if you can't lay deep enough foundations at the outset—which is arguably the basic issue in the current attempt to bring peace to Iraq. It is also much more difficult to prop up a shaky edifice at a later date.

Like a well-established set of architectural rules, which everyone assents to and upholds, the American Constitution has defined the shape and set the style of the great national 'home' that has been built over the past two centuries: a house of liberty, in which individuals are encouraged and empowered to take the opportunities available to them—and to create more. It has fostered a diverse commercial competitiveness, welcoming enterprise and innovation without any fear that they might threaten the security it has created. Indeed, it harks back to the Declaration of Independence and the fundamental rights and ideals that that expressed, which provided Abraham Lincoln with the ideological and political resources to dismantle the institution of slavery in the 19th century and gave King's Civil Rights movement the leverage to overturn racial segregation in the 20th. It was the thinking in those first, foundational statements that was the scaffolding in which the 'architecture' of America took shape in the centuries that followed. Likewise, the feeling of confidence and cultural 'belonging' that these foundational ideals engender, as well as the festivals and rites of passage associated with them, endow Americans with a strong sense of national identity. In no British city (and few European cities) will you see the national flag hanging in school yards and the windows of private homes— except during the World Cup—or find schoolchildren beginning their day singing the national anthem or reciting the national civic constitution.[1] Outside Switzerland and Scandinavia, 21st-century Europeans lack the same sense of collective national identity.

## Social foundations create limits

What foundations provide for the building above them—whether it is a suburban home or a shopping centre or a skyscraper—is a basis on which people can live safely and securely, without anxiety. Belief in the liberty of the individual, freedom of expression, the right to happiness, these values have supported and sustained an economy that has dominated the world since the Second World War. The economy of Europe, while not as powerful, is built on the same values of individual enterprise, the free flow of capital and the right of the individual to create and amass personal wealth. The free-market capitalism of both America and northern Europe owes much of its character to the Protestant work ethic that underlies it and, with its emphasis on hard work, self-discipline and the renunciation of immediate pleasure for the sake of profit to come, gives it spiritual and moral strength. The same ethic asserts both the responsibility of the individual to learn, grow and make the most of their God-given opportunities and gifts and, at the same time, the subordination of the individual to the authorities set over them, whether church or state, which it sees as agents and instruments of God's ordering of this world. Western industrial society is built on the twin premises of the capacity of the individual to create wealth and the authority of the state to constrain behaviour. The result has been dynamic economic growth but within the bounds of shared moral and cultural values—in other words, freedom within limits.

## The weakening of our social foundations

However, over the past century there has been a concerted and quite aggressive attempt on both sides of the Atlantic to undermine the social and moral foundations that have sustained our societies. This endeavour owes its origins

---

[1] 'Whilst some nations promote the national flag and other symbols of nationhood through education, there has been no recent tradition of flag flying and the singing of a national anthem in schools in England' Hugh Starkey, Jeremy Hayward and Karen Turner, 'Education for Citizenship', *Reflecting Education*, 2 (2) (2006), p2. Retrieved on 8 March 2008 from http://reflectingeducation.net/index.php?journal=reflecting&page=article&op=view&path%5B%5D=31&path%5B%5D=31

to many things, but one that has almost symbolic significance was a debate that took place in 1863 in my home city of Oxford. This event had such powerful intellectual consequences, it could be compared to an earthquake that shook the very foundations of a whole society— an earthquake whose aftershocks are still being felt to this day.

In 1859, Charles Darwin published his book *On the Origin of Species*.[2] In it, he set out the hypothesis that all the diversity of life on earth could be accounted for by a process he called 'natural selection'. While he himself did not suggest that such an explanation debunked or even doubted the idea that the world and everything on it were made by an omnipotent, divine Creator, the church at the time understood it as an attack on the biblical account of creation in the Book of Genesis. Instead of seeking to understand the new theory, the church tried to demolish it. In June 1860, Samuel Wilberforce, the then bishop of Oxford, invited the biologist Thomas Huxley to debate Darwin's ideas with him. Their encounter took place in a room on the top floor of the University's museum of natural history and, though many accounts are clearly mythic, undoubtedly resulted in a decisive victory for Huxley. It became clear that no good case could be made against Darwin's theory on the basis of scientific evidence alone.

This controversy contributed to an emerging consensus in our culture that it might be more expedient to regard hard, empirical science and matters of faith as existing in different epistemological worlds. In one, truth was established by rational research; in the other, by personal experience and belief. The crucial outcome of the debate was the detachment of science from any foundations of religious faith. Science, people began to think, offered a more comprehensive account of the world than Christianity and did not need the support of religious dogma. Indeed, religion was in competition with truth, not an avenue to it. One almost immediate result of this development was that the church began to retreat from intellectual life, wounded by this and other experiences of its authority being questioned. If you visit Oxford today, you will see that opposite the University's natural history museum stands Keble College. Built just a few years after the debate between Wilberforce and Huxley, it was founded by and named after John Keble, who, with others in the so-called Oxford Movement, mounted something of a religious resistance to the 'secularization' they saw around them.

However, this resistance was not primarily intellectual, nor did it seek to re-enter the debates, scientific, literary and historical, that had already been lost. Instead, it tended to define religious faith in terms of a personal, experiential

---

[2] Charles Darwin, *On the Origin of Species by Means of Natural Selection: or, The Preservation of Favoured Races in the Struggle for Life* (London: J Murray, 1859)

moral piety and inner spirituality that need have no connection to the outer, intellectual world. In essence, it defended the sacred by removing it from the secular. The Christian faith had been protected, but at great cost—closeted away in a safe corner where believers could hold on to their own personal faith and morality without having to engage in the turmoil of debate going on in the commercial, cultural, intellectual and political life of the nation.[3] Meanwhile, science steadily became established as a new quasi-religion, and with evangelistic zeal its ministers of truth began to reform school and university curricula up and down the land.

As a graduate in biological sciences from Oxford myself, I come down firmly on the side of Huxley in the debate with Wilberforce, whose arguments I believe were false and unsustainable. However, I believe that something crucial was lost when Huxley demolished the church's credibility, and that was the link between the market and morality. If the church and its notion of individual responsibility but subordination to church and state were no longer to guide public life, what else was going to? What was to emerge over the next hundred years was a new principle: the freedom of the individual subordinated only to the limits of technology. In the absence of any moral rule derived from theology, British society rapidly began to explore novel social mores. Permissiveness—legal, sexual and intellectual—became an essential element of modern liberal democracy. In the market, a new breed of entrepreneurs and 'captains of industry' emerged who lacked any overriding commitment to social cohesion. In science, debates about genetic modification, IVF, embryo growth, human cloning, abortion, euthanasia and the environment have been conducted by technocrats who have lacked a coherent moral framework to shape their decision making. Consequently legislation made by one body contradicts that made by another. Because there is no agreed view on the value of human life, the right to an abortion is promulgated alongside the right to IVF—with one hand our society takes life, with the other it gives it. Because we have no shared perspective on death, demands for the right to have our lives extended by medical science if the means are available are mingled with calls for

---

[3] The major initiatives of the Christian church in the West in the last century have focused on either social or personal mission. The former has usually been conducted through agencies designed to support those who have fallen out of society's safety net—drug users, homeless people, sex workers, people who have been abused. Often, this has involved remarkable (and unsung) commitment outside the structures of politics and government in what is now called the 'third' or 'voluntary' sector of our economy. Personal mission has taken the form of initiatives, large and small, to communicate the message of the Christian faith and demand a personal response. Examples are the Billy Graham 'Crusades' of the 1950s and '60s, the Church of England's 'Decade of Evangelism' in the 1980s and the Alpha movement of the 1990s onwards. Their 'call to conversion' has always focused on personal piety but has rarely emphasized either the need or the means to contribute to the reshaping of our culture. As a result, three generations of Christians have been involved largely in saving individuals in one sense or the other but not in transforming nations.

euthanasia to be legalized as more and more of us limp on into advanced old age. Because we have no common understanding of the nature of personhood, we are busily creating designer embryos even as we seek to protect our rights to personal privacy and integrity. Our law-making is pulled in contradictory directions by our commitment to individual rights and freedoms as opposed to any social or religious commitment.

## *Freedom without limits*

To be simplistic, the West in the 20th century could be summed up in one sentence: 'Because we can, we will.' Given the fantastic ability of our technology to open up, it seems, ever new sources of power, whether medical, military or commercial, we appear to have found no way of saying 'No'. Because we can, we will. However, just because we can does not mean that we must. Because we can does not mean necessarily that we want to. There is a moral choice. We don't have to develop the technology. But, now we have detached morality from the marketplace, the reality has been that whenever a commercial case can be made for some technological advance, sooner or later that advance will be exploited. Sometimes it has taken a while before we have gone through the opened door, but almost every door that has been opened, in medicine, entertainment or whatever, we have gone through in the end. The same is true in other areas of human endeavour—for example, in artistic expression.

The West has almost no moral mechanism for saying 'No' any more—and that is a terrifying situation for a society to be in, because it is only a small step from being unable to say no to breaking down completely. Émile Durkheim coined the term 'anomie' for the condition of a society in which social and moral norms are confused or missing altogether.[4] He argued that, whereas traditional societies managed to teach people (primarily through religion) to control their desires and aspirations, modern industrial societies tend to separate people and so weaken social bonds, and this has the effect of removing such constraints. Whereas people's desires and aspirations previously were curbed by social order and morality, now they seem to know no limit.[5] Inevitably, cracks have begun to

---

[4] 'Anomie springs from the lack of collective forces at certain points in society; that is, of groups established for the regulation of social life': Émile Durkheim, *Suicide: A Study in Sociology* (this translation, J A Spaulding and G Simpson, London: Routledge & Kegan Paul, 1952), p382. See also p258. The book was published originally in 1897.

[5] 'The third sort of suicide ... results from man's activity's lacking regulation and his consequent sufferings. By virtue of its origin we shall assign this last variety the name of anomic suicide. ... In anomic suicide, society's influence is lacking in the basically individual passions, thus leaving them without a check-rein': Ibid., p258

'Religion has lost most of its power. ... Industry ... has become the supreme end of individuals and societies alike. Thereupon the appetites thus excited have become freed of any limiting authority': Ibid., p255

appear in the social edifice that was once supported by a foundation of shared values, and it has started to collapse.

It is the lack of such a constraining 'architecture' that has allowed the unprecedented, unregulated growth in our industries and our exploitation of the world's resources. Take, for example, our energy consumption. Five years ago, the average American was using nearly 24 times as much energy as the average Indian.[6] It has been estimated by some researchers that it would take at least six Earths to support the current global population at such levels of consumption.[7] The situation is simply unsustainable, and there is no question that within 30 years we will all have to reduce our consumption—not least because the global population is projected to have risen by another two billion by then!

Similarly, the systemic failure of the 'architecture' of our financial regulatory structures has allowed the unprecedentedly irresponsible leverage of global debt. What was needed to hold our personal freedoms in reasonable check, as Durkheim stressed a hundred years ago, was the constraint of foundational shared values that would have governed our individual appetites for comfort and convenience.

## *Social foundations reduce the burden on the individual*

In dismantling the morality of our society, and allowing unbounded individual freedom on what I have called 'the front stage', the liberal capitalist agenda has inadvertently created a social system that has no mechanism of self-regulation. Ultimately, the individual consumer has to regulate herself if any capitalist system is to be sustained. What our economy requires is not just financial capital, or a more robust structure of financial regulations, but the social capital of self-restraint and a morality that considers the consequences of our actions for others, even if they are invisible to us on the other side of the world. It requires a willingness to curb our appetites, as well as confidence in a self-identity that is not defined simply by how much we own and how much we consume. Without these personal, psychological foundations in place, the Western edifice was always going to become unstable. The sheer scale of the global economic crisis

---

[6] 'India's per capita annual energy consumption was 594kWh in 2003 compared with 14,057kWh in the US': Amy Yee, 'Flood Threat to Bangladesh a Warning to the World', *The Financial Times*, 2 February 2007, p9

[7] 'It is only fair that other nations would want access to the same types of homes, education, cars, health and luxury consumables that we enjoy. The problem is that this type of global consumption is not possible. It would take more than six planets with the same resource supplies as [E]arth in order to sustain a global suburban lifestyle': *Peak Oil News*, 6 November 2006 (http://www.peak-oil-news.info/north-american-energy-consumption)

bears witness to the yawning holes that for the past 30 years have been opening up under many Western economies and societies.

## Social foundations locate and support society

One of the ways in which the crumbling of our society's foundations has affected us is in the collapse of our shared cultural disciplines and patterns. The loss of daily, weekly and annual rhythms of life, both personal and national, has been a feature of the past two decades, accelerated by the opportunities of our globalized economy. In a market operating across time zones, diurnal rhythms necessarily become less marked. The same is true for annual rhythms as supermarkets offer us strawberries in January and clementines in June and cut-price air travel makes the summer sun accessible all year. Television—in particular, satellite TV—lets us watch seasonal sports at any time of year, while all-weather pitches and floodlights have lifted the restrictions on when we can watch games live. Urbanization has reduced our contact with the rhythms of nature, and our air-conditioned cars remove us from the vagaries of the weather. In Britain specifically the Sunday Trading Act of 1989 abolished the one day off a week that everyone had shared, while European Union regulations now insist on an indiscriminate 48-hour week. Shift work, flexitime, overtime and home working all have the effect of flattening the demographically shared rhythm.[8] Meanwhile, 24-hour news channels, all-night television and the 'omnitemporality' of the internet mean a world always on the go. We have become trapped in an accelerating treadmill of economic expansionism from which we are unwilling to escape.

In addition, the benefit of the old rhythms lay in giving a sense of shape to our lives. For example, the discipline of not buying anything on a Sunday reminded us that shopping is not all there is to life. Instead, that one day a week could be reserved for other activities as a family, a community or (for some) a church—a practice that more secular but arguably more family-orientated European societies such as France and Germany retain.

The foundations of a society include a shared rhythm and a shared calendar. Feast days and fast days tell a shared story and both express and reinforce a society's self-identity and sense of cohesion. They also inculcate personal discipline and foster a sense of anticipation. However, the West has lost confidence in the legitimacy of celebrating Christmas, Easter, Whitsun (or Pentecost) and All Saints' Day as specifically Christian festivals (for fear of alienating adherents

---

[8] 'Organisation of Working Time (Basic Directive)', directive 2003/88/EC of the European Parliament and the Council of 4 November 2003, retrieved on 10 March 2008 from http://europa.eu/scadplus/leg/en/cha/c10418.htm

of other faiths) and instead these occasions have been exploited merely as commercial opportunities. Our sacrifice of a shared religious story has created not a richer cultural environment but a poorer one—except in financial terms. The same can be said of the erosion of social conviction about other cultural markers (such as Remembrance Sunday) and their historical origins by the guilt we feel about our nation's past. When such shared stories are forgotten or disregarded, society fragments. It is difficult to resist the impulse towards individualism—an individualism that increasingly has defined itself through insatiable acquisition and consumption.

## *Loss of social foundations inspires contempt*

In 1964, while living in America, the Egyptian scholar Sayyid Qutb was provoked by that 'open and free' land to write *Milestones*.[9] We should take notice of this, because the book inspired the modern jihad movement. Qutb had devoured Oswald Spengler's *Decline of the West*, Arnold Toynbee's *A Study of History* and T S Eliot's *The Waste Land*, which all portrayed the West as degenerate and profane, lacking any direction. He found in this a parallel to the state of depravity and godlessness that had existed in Arabia before the arrival of the Prophet Muhammad, and he called on his readers to destroy 'this rubbish heap of the West'. Critics will say that Qutb misread those writers and that the West was neither degenerate nor profane. However, when we consider the dynamics of social ecology we see that there is more truth in his perception than we would like to admit.

A society that has no shared values, a market that has lost touch with morality, is a terrifying place to be in. It is fundamentally unsafe, like a building without firm foundations. Its collapse is only a matter of time. Technology cannot itself provide the foundational limits because it has no limits itself. Science will continue to advance, and ever more powerful cures will be invented because the market will demand them. It is also true that ever more powerful bombs will be invented, because the market will demand them, too. Technology, always and only morally neutral, takes no account of its social consequences, good or evil. It can only—and must be—constrained by a moral discourse that lies outside the realm and the control of the scientist and the technocrat. The only alternative is to put our fate entirely in the hands of those who simply hold most power.

Technology was sufficient to overcome the chaotic forces of nature; it could impose its own order on the disorder of the world. The myth of technology as a means of government and social order is always seductive: we are captivated by

---

[9] Sayyid Qutb, *Milestones* (this edition, Beirut: The Holy Koran Publishing House, 1980)

the extraordinary, mesmeric promises of a better and brighter future in a world free of disease and poverty—if only we can make this or that technological breakthrough. We in the West readily subordinate ourselves to the authority and the promises of the technocrats and the free-market economists who want to build and govern our world on the basis of 'Because we can, we will,' who believe that the market will regulate itself. My concern is that we won't stop until we can't go on—and then it will be too late.

## *Study questions 2*

1. What are some of the deepest foundations in your own society?
2. In what ways are these currently being eroded or undermined?
3. What are the implications if that continues?
4. What lessons about social foundations can we learn from recent Western history?

# THREE

## The Insatiable Hunger of the Well-Fed (PWX)

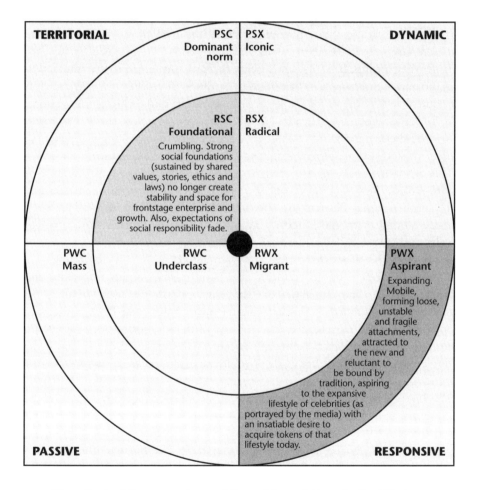

The effect of the current crumbling of foundations in the West on aspirational behaviour

**Chapter summary**

In this chapter, we explore the Aspirant sector of the social ecology model, which I have given the code PWX. These letters stand for *'presented'*, *'weak'* and *'expanding'*.

'Presented' refers to an element in society that is visible, explicit and on public view, and perhaps no aspect of our society is so obvious, so 'presented', as our aspirational consumerism! Almost the first thing that most people see when they arrive in the West is the shops in the airport terminal—and their drive from the airport will then take them past out-of-town shopping precincts and 'retail parks'. We live surrounded by opportunities to purchase and consume.

At the same time, our consumption is highly responsive to the market's leading. It tends to react to the opportunities placed in front of it rather than being directed by a proactive set of values. In other words, it responds by weak force rather than strong. It is inherently open, receptive, attracted to the stimulation of the new and reluctant to be bound by tradition or earlier norms. We see this in our society's hunger for the latest fashions, styles and technical innovations, as consumers gobble up the new 'goodies' that are set before them. The menu is set by the designers and researchers who, alert to the developing appetites of their markets, extract money from us by catering for our desires.

This element in society also tends to sacrifice those things that stabilize, or consolidate, our society in favour of those that expand our horizons and add to our possessions. Physical and emotional flexibility and mobility are favoured above commitment and longevity. Goods are discarded rather than repaired. Relationships are ended rather than endured.

If we combine these three elements—presented, weak and expanding—we identify an element in our culture that is highly visible, highly responsive and highly mobile. These qualities are the exact opposite of the Foundational qualities we examined in the last chapter, just as the code PWX is the very opposite of RSC. The characteristic features of the foundations of a society are entirely absent from its consumerist aspirations – and vice versa. It is as if the very erosion of the RSC has made possible the explosion of the PWX. The two trends seem to have developed in concert.

This highlights a crucial dynamic of this model of social ecology, which can be expressed simply like this: any action has an equal and opposite reaction. Our social ecology behaves like a closed system: any movement or pressure in one part of it produces a commensurate movement or pressure in another part. It's rather like a balloon half full of air—when you squeeze it at one end, it tends to bulge at the other. Your inward pressure at one point applies an outward force elsewhere.

This feature of the model of social ecology is one of its most important and illuminating, as it enables us to predict what the response will be to any pressure we apply. In this instance, the two related sectors of the model are PWX and RSC. As the RSC foundations of our society have been eroded or have crumbled, so its PWX aspirations have been expanded.

## Summary statement

*Detached from the constraints exerted by strong foundations, our aspirational behaviour has become insatiable and unregulated. The consequences of this are psychological fragility, social insecurity, financial debt and a lack of cultural resilience.*

...................................................

Building sandcastles may be a peculiarly British pastime. The vicissitudes of our weather have made us experts at making the most of a grey and sometimes rainy outing to the beach, and building sandcastles is something you will find countless families doggedly engaged in on a typical summer day by the sea. One reason why it is so satisfying, of course, is that it can take only a few minutes of furious digging, piling and moulding before you have a respectable structure in front of you. And not just a castle keep: there may also be a moat and a drawbridge, turrets, battlements, even lookout holes and booby traps and other features of an embattled community.

Of course, the enemy you are fighting is not a raiding force from another castle but the sea itself. For while the whole edifice can be constructed in an hour or so, it may take only a matter of minutes for the returning tide to wash it away entirely, for all the industry and imagination that went into it. In the end, building sandcastles is an exercise in futility. However, that very fact only spurs the builders to greater effort, and even as the tide is remorselessly coming in, they are devising ingenious and optimistic schemes to divert it with walls and ditches in order to preserve the castle for as long as possible. They know the inevitable outcome, but they choose to suspend their disbelief and think that they might, miraculously, against all odds, find a way to defy the elements. Building sandcastles is an exercise in fragility. By definition, it is building without foundations. The advantages are that you can build quickly and expansively— and can 'make it up as you go along'; the downside is that, inevitably, all you construct lacks solidity and strength—a few waves will wash it away.

If it is true that over the past century the West has assiduously undermined its own social, moral and cultural foundations, it will also, worryingly, be true that the edifices that are now standing stand on sand and not rock. One would expect to see alarming signs of fragility at various levels: in the emotional and psychological well-being of individuals, the social and relational health of marriages and communities, the energy and engagement in political life and the resilience of the economy.

## *Psychological fragility*

One of the key foundations of our society in the past was the accepted permanence of marriage. Regarded as both divinely ordained and the appropriate environment within which to bring children into the world and nurture them, this was one of the strongest sources of social cohesion until the middle of the 20th century. Since then, this part of our social foundations has been systematically deconstructed. To many people today, it is no more than a quaint—and deeply restrictive—convention. Similarly, many people see the idea that 'sexual union' is a sign to society of the formation of a new, discrete and permanent social unit as archaic and irrelevant. Finally, the notion that it is healthier for children to be raised in such an environment has been attacked ferociously for the last three decades by many intellectuals who argue that any number and variety of sexual attachments, long or short, are good enough—or even preferable.

Once we had lost the conviction that sexual union, accompanied by responsibility and commitment, is integral to social cohesion, it was inevitable that social bonding was going to become more fluid and fleeting. This was facilitated, of course, by the invention of the Pill, and given extra impetus by a reaction in the 1960s against the repressive mores of the post-Victorian era. As a result, whereas once most people, adults and children, enjoyed strong and stable attachments, today, with their sexual and emotional boundaries largely open, people experience each other as available, as convenient and expedient. Any people who see themselves in this way become insecure, unsure of the reliability of relationships. Commitment becomes increasingly difficult; unattached sex becomes an anxious surrogate for intimacy, a panacea for loneliness—and yet it cannot provide the social or emotional 'anchorage' of an enduring relationship. In purely medical terms, there is a dramatic rise in the incidence of both sexually transmitted diseases (STDs) and, some evidence suggests (as a result of delayed childbirth and multiple sexual partners), infertility.[10] However, the most profound effects have been on children.

---

[10] 'Between 1991 and 2001, the number of new episodes of sexually transmitted infections (STIs) seen in Genitourinary Medicine (GUM) clinics in England, Wales and Northern Ireland doubled from 669,291 to 1,332,910. Young people, in particular females under the age of 20, bear the burden of sexually transmitted infections. ... The sexual health of adolescents in the UK is poor. It is likely that an increase in risky sexual behaviour has contributed to sexual health outcomes such as STIs and unwanted pregnancy among young people': 'Sexual Health: Teen Infection Almost Doubled during 90s', National Statistics, 30 March 2004. Retrieved on 27 March 2008 from http://www.statistics.gov.uk/cci/nugget.asp?id=721

## *A growing social cost*

After two generations of children have experienced the open boundaries of emotional and sexual mobility, we have a legacy of growing emotional dysfunction.[11] Developmental psychologists agree on the cause of this: when a child is unable to trust the relationship between his caregivers, he will, inevitably, find other ways to cope with his lack of security. Emotional 'self-holding' (which manifests itself in anxiety, depression, self-harm and aggression) and emotional incontinence (attention seeking, lack of impulse control, proneness to distraction) alike are, unsurprisingly, characteristic of an 'unboundaried' population.[12] This is what we must expect, increasingly, from children who have experienced adult relationships as both unpredictable and fragile. The incidence of such dysfunctions has risen dramatically in the past decade.[13] The extraordinary rise of ADHD (attention-deficit and hyperactive disorder) in recent years, though caused by a mix of factors from processed foods to patterns of parenting to the advent of TV remotes and game consoles, suggests that the context in which children now grow up is essentially one in which change is the only thing that is predictable.[14]

---

[11] 'Nearly a quarter (24 per cent) of children in Great Britain were living in lone-parent families in 2006, more than three times the proportion in 1972': 'Changing Lives of Today's Children', National Statistics 2007 news release regarding the 37th edition of *Social Trends*. Retrieved on 10 March 2008 from http://www.statistics.gov.uk/pdfdir/st0407.pdf

[12] 'Half those children with a mental disorder had at one time seen the separation of their parents, compared with 29 per cent with no disorder': 'Mental Health of Children and Adolescents', ONS (2000) 118. Retrieved on 27 March 2008 from http://www.statistics.gov.uk/pdfdir/mhc0300.pdf. 'Family stability is positively related to child and young adult behavior (Hao & Xie, 2001; Hill et al., 2001; Wu & Martinson, 1993)': W D Manning and K A Lamb, 'Adolescent Well-Being in Cohabiting, Married, and Single-Parent Families', *Journal of Marriage and Family* 65 (2003), pp876–93. However, other authors consider other factors that contribute to social problems: 'Poverty, abuse, neglect, poorly funded schools, and a lack of government services represent more serious threats to the well-being of adults and children than does marital instability': P R Amato, 'The Consequences of Divorce for Adults and Children', *Journal of Marriage and the Family* 62 (2000), pp1269–87

[13] 'A recent study based on information from the GP Research Database found that between 1991 and 2001, the rate of British children prescribed antidepressants rose by 70%. In the US, a pandemic is already in progress. One out of every six American children, according to a recent declaration of the House Committee on Energy and Commerce, is taking a prescription antidepressant such as Prozac': John Cornwell, 'Prozac for Eight-Year-Olds?', *The Sunday Times*, 12 November 2006, p14

[14] 'Of the disturbed 10%, half have behavioural problems, 40% anxiety or depression, 15% attention-deficit hyperactivity disorder (ADHD), and 8% autistic spectrum disorders (some children have multiple problems). ... Everyone has their pet explanation—lack of fish oil, TV-watching, illegal drugs, lack of exercise. Likely candidates in [Professor Robert] Goodman's eyes are widening inequality, family breakdown, school pressures and a materialist, consumerist society. ... "Both behaviour and ADHD are much worse in Britain. Norwegians live in a much more equal society, with shorter working days, more time spent with families, particularly on outdoor sports at weekends, public values publicly shared. They eat lots of oily fish, too!"': Victoria Neumark, 'Education: Wellbeing and the Web', *The Guardian*, 15 January 2008, p29

The British government has implemented a raft of initiatives to try to tackle such problems: basic training in parenting, school counsellors, an entire curriculum of 'emotional literacy' in schools across the country.[15] In essence, it is trying to teach adults skills they never learnt from their parents, and to use schools to nurture their children because their families are so fragile and dysfunctional. It seems that the cost of undermining our society's moral foundations has been high. Has it been worth it? The argument has always been that those sexual and domestic morals were restrictive and denied individuals freedom of choice; people were unhappy being stuck in marriages after love had died. But has the removal of those old 'Victorian' constraints made us happier? Sadly, it seems not. Measures of overall well-being in Britain suggest that people are no more content today than they were 50 years ago.[16] In other words, our society is no happier despite its new freedoms. However, it now sees a far higher incidence of mental-health problems: depression, anxiety disorders, stress-related problems and suicide, in particular among young males.[17]

## *Social mobility and social fragility*

We are now physically mobile to a degree the world has never known before. The mass manufacture of cars and motorbikes, increases in oil production and cheap air travel have all given us the ability and opportunity to roam far afield. At the same time, we have witnessed a corresponding change in our cultural attitudes that has made it acceptable, and even desirable, to leave behind the place you grew up in in pursuit of employment—or fulfilment—unfettered by local attachments.

In Britain, this mobility was greatly encouraged in the 1970s by the social policy of Margaret Thatcher's Conservative government. Social housing, which the state had owned in the inner cities through local councils, was sold off at the insistence of an ideology that believed that people would aspire to improve themselves only if they owned their own homes. The results have been nothing less than spectacular. The average price of a house in Britain has gone

---

[15] 'Respect Drive Targets Troublesome Families', Department of Health news release, 10 January 2006 (http://www.dh.gov.uk/en/publicationsandstatistics/pressreleases/dh_4126269); 'Better Support for Emotional Wellbeing in Schools—25 Pilot Areas Announced', Department for Children, Schools and Families news release, 24 January 2008 (http://www.dcsf.gov.uk/pns/DisplayPN.cgi?pn_id=2008_0016)

[16] 'Britain's Happiness in Decline', Mark Easton, BBC News, 2 May 2006 (http://news.bbc.co.uk/1/hi/programmes/happiness_formula/4771908.stm)

[17] 'Mental Health: Mental Disorders More Common in Boys', National Statistics, 30 March 2004. Retrieved on 1 April 2008 from http://www.statistics.gov.uk/cci/nugget.asp?id=853

up 3,900 per cent between 1971 and 2007,[18] while monetary inflation has barely exceeded 900 per cent.[19] The early consequence of the policy was that large parts of many British cities were emptied of their indigenous populations as people sold their recently acquired council flats and houses and moved out (and up) into the suburbs or newly-built towns.

The mass ownership of cars has opened up a far larger landscape that has been exploited by commerce in several ways. Large, cheap out-of-town stores and shopping centres have proved very popular, but take us away from our local shops. The fragility of employment contracts means that people's working patterns are necessarily more fluid—and precarious.[20] Often, people will commute long distances, returning home only late in the evening. Indeed, 'home' is arguably a misnomer—T S Eliot's references to a 'homeless' city and suburb in which God therefore finds no home now seem not only apt but prophetic.[21] This increase of our physical mobility has corresponded with an emotional and cultural mobility, as people are no longer so tied to a particular world view, set of values, aspirations and economic prospects.

## Social mobility and social isolation

In emotional terms, family roots have never been so confused. In 1995, there were 165,000 divorces in Britain, 280 times the number in the first year of the century.[22] Today, over half of the population under 40 has been affected by divorce, whether as parents or as children. According to the social psychologist Oliver James, the consequent emotional havoc has been appalling.[23] The arrival on the scene of further partners after a parental break-up increases a child's confusion and is likely to affect her emotional development badly.

What has occurred demographically has been legitimized intellectually. Individualism was a hallmark of Enlightenment thinking,[24] and postmodernism, though it rejects much of the modernist agenda, is perhaps better referred to as 'hyper-modernism' when it comes to its approach to the individual.

---

[18] http://www.communities.gov.uk/housing/housingresearch/housingstatistics/housingstatisticsby/housingmarket/livetables

[19] http://www.measuringworth.com/ppoweruk/result.php?use%5b%5d=cpi&year_late=1971&typeamount=1000&amount=1000&year_source=1971&year_result=2007

[20] See David Harvey, *The Condition of Postmodernity: an Enquiry into the Origins of Cultural Change* (Blackwell, 1989), p303 on the economic drivers of, and postmodern confusion about and quest for, roots.

[21] 'Choruses from *The Rock*', T S Eliot, *Collected Poems, 1909–1962* (Faber and Faber, 1968), p162

[22] Oliver James, *Britain on the Couch* (Century, 1997), p152

[23] Ibid., p157

[24] J Richard Middleton and Brian J Walsh, *Truth Is Stranger Than It Used To Be* (SPCK, 1995), p47

Psychologically, we find ourselves playing roles, not rediscovering our roots. As the social psychologist Kenneth Gergen put it: 'Since there is no essential me, I can be whoever I want to be.'[25] Postmodern Man is 'able to be anything so long as the roles, costumes, and settings have been commodiously arranged.'[26]

A mobile society quickly becomes a society in which people are isolated and find they lack neighbours, friends and family nearby who they can turn to when in need. Isolation then turns to anonymity, as people feel less and less 'known' by or 'connected' with their local communities. Their sense of belonging diminishes and, rather than gaining a sense of identity and well-being through social ties, people turn to acquisition and consumption as ways to define themselves and 'belong' to some group. In this way, we are commoditized and lose our sense of depth, place and history as we focus instead on the brand of clothing we wear or the car we drive. Economically, our society's fragmentation puts unprecedented pressure on the housing stock as the total number of 'housing units' spirals to meet the needs of people living more and more solitary lives.[27]

## *Growing economic fragility*

Perhaps the single biggest economic change over the past three decades has involved the financing mechanisms now available to the consumer. We now borrow money not within the local community (or the family) but outside it, unconstrained by social ties. Before the Second World War, debt was socially stigmatized. Generally, people borrowed from a member of their family or the local community—perhaps a pawnbroker or a loan shark—and in such a system it was seen as an expensive last resort that could eat up both capital and reputation. The social pressure to repay a loan was often immense. Today, in contrast, huge, remote, impersonal banks provide 'credit' without any stigma attached—in fact, often they offer it unsolicited and present this as a compliment! There is usually no pressure to settle your debts—indeed, repayment even of large unsecured loans can now be spread over many years, something unheard of only 20 years ago. Vast amounts of credit are now available as a result, and all without social stigma.

With the means to finance aspiration now in place, the full-scale swelling of this sector of the population can take place. A population insecure about personal identity seeks fulfilment in the acquisition of branded 'lifestyle' goods, which

---

[25] Ibid., p53
[26] Ibid., quoting Kenneth Gergen, p53
[27] 'In 2004 there were 7.0 million people living alone in Great Britain, nearly four times as many as in 1961': 'Households: More People Were Living Alone in 2004', National Statistics, 2005 (http://www.statistics.gov.uk/cci/nugget.asp?id=1162&pos=&colrank=2&rank=672)

act as surrogates for tradition and a sense of social identity. We can now invent and reinvent our own stories through our clothes and accessories. In effect, the easy availability of credit furnishes the 'front stage' of our personal theatres with costumes, props, narratives and scripts—all of which are disposable. We now have a plethora of lifestyles from which to choose, and when we become bored we can simply move on to a different costume, a different drama, even a different cast of co-actors. Our physical, emotional and social mobility mean we can now give our technologically-navigated virtual lives whatever shape or form we need to pull the illusion off.

And in all of this we consume. Our ever-expanding storylines get through enormous quantities of goods. The fashions we embrace literally label us amidst the chaos of fleeting encounters in which we now engage. Brands are now deliberately promoted as the new traditions, which help to give us a shape to our narrative and a sense of community.[28] Our appetites are insatiable simply because the function for which we buy each costume or prop in the first place— to set ourselves within some bigger drama devised by other people—is itself only transitory and illusory.

And of course such consumption is unsustainable. Britain's consumer debt (including mortgages) now totals £1.4 trillion.[29] America's (excluding mortgages) is nearly $14 trillion,[30] or over $20,000 for every household, and its trade deficit is now $58 billion.[31] We dress our lack of identity at a terrible and unsustainable price not only to our social ecology, our economies, but also to our planet. And it does not lead to a happier society. The market works by creating desires that are fulfilled only briefly, in order to sustain relentless demand. As Durkheim observed in his work *Suicide,* 'To pursue a goal which is by definition unattainable is to condemn oneself to a state of perpetual unhappiness.'[32] Thus, we find that the incidence of depression and mental disease in our society has never been higher.

---

[28] 'Material goods are important to us, not just for their functional uses, but because they play vital symbolic roles in our lives. This symbolic role of consumer goods facilitates a range of complex, deeply engrained "social conversations" about status, identity, social cohesion, group norms and the pursuit of personal and cultural meaning': Tim Jackson, 'Motivating Sustainable Consumption: A Review of Evidence on Consumer Behaviour and Behavioural Change' (draft version), 1 August 2004 (http://portal.surrey.ac.uk/pls/portal/docs/page/eng/staff/staffac/jacksont/publications/jacksonsdrn-review.pdf)

[29] J Charles, 'Debt Watch', *The Times,* 22 March 2008, p16

[30] Paul Harris, 'Living on Borrowed Dimes', *The Guardian,* 4 May 2006. Retrieved on 1 April 2008 from http://www.guardian.co.uk/business/2006/may/04/usnews.comment; 'American household debt reached $13.8 trillion at the end of 2007, or more than double the amount in 1999': 'America's Coming Garage Sale', *Time,* 24 March 2008 (http://www.time.com/time/magazine/article/0,9171,1725094,00.html)

[31] 'Goods and Services Deficit Increases in January 2008', US Census Bureau, 11 March 2008 (http://www.census.gov/indicator/www/ustrade.html)

[32] Op. cit., p248

The sheer fragility of our financial system is now being exposed. The scale of the collapse of the real economies of some countries will be so great simply because the tolerances in people's domestic finances are so tight. Leveraged to the hilt with both secured and unsecured debt, a steep rise in unemployment or fall in property values will plunge millions into financial crisis. Retailers, reliant on consumer spending, will go into liquidation. Brands will disappear. Whole economies may become bankrupt. Future generations will look back at us and ask how we ever could have believed we could carry on consuming the way we have done.

## Political fragility

Tragically, one reason is that in Britain and America—and perhaps in the West more generally—there has been a systemic failure of political leadership over the past 20 years, caused specifically by a dereliction of the basic, essential contract between governments and the people they govern. In a democracy, political leadership is based on a social contract. Citizens willingly submit to the laws made by their elected representatives and, in so doing, recognize that they are responsible participants in the social system, not simply individuals at liberty to do what they please. However, as Durkheim suggests in the observation quoted above, this requires us to rein our appetites in. The problem in the West is that our politicians have increasingly seen themselves as corporate managers and us as consumers of their 'products'.

Politics is increasingly concerned with offering us a range of 'choices' as consumers, rather than with presenting us with our responsibilities as citizens. Pollsters and focus-group researchers have done their work and have found that when you ask people they will always demand greater freedom of choice in their own lives. But a politics that expects governments simply to satisfy the demands of consumers in order to win another term in power is a politics not worth having. The result is that politicians are afraid to demand any genuine personal sacrifice in the interests of greater collective good. It is tragic to see education and health policies designed to offer us greater choice rather than greater commitment to our neighbourhood and its resources. Why should anyone commit themselves to improving their local schools and hospital if they can just choose to go further afield to get treatment or education somewhere else? What will happen to the schools and hospitals that those who can afford to go elsewhere abandon?

## *A less resilient society*

Detaching a society from its historic foundations is a costly business. Although it may seem to offer individuals freedom and opportunity to express themselves, ultimately it exposes them to powerful forces they will be unable to resist. The population in general becomes more fragile psychologically as each generation of broken families leaves a growing legacy to the next. The social fabric becomes thinner and more tattered; individuals become more isolated and more anonymous as they become more mobile, and increasingly define their sense of identity through the brands they wear rather than the families, communities and friendship groups they belong to. Economically, such a society slides into a debt culture in order to finance its over-consumption. Aspiration ceases to have any social worth because people aspire to have things that can neither satisfy them in the long term nor help to build a cohesive society. Politically, people regard themselves increasingly as consumers rather than citizens, and politicians offer the electorate a choice of products rather than privileges on the basis of shared responsibilities. Political discourse descends into arguments about rights and becomes increasingly litigious.

Those who benefit from these changes are the people who finance consumer debt, negotiate legal contracts and sell consumers the goods they demand in order to define themselves. The economy grows rapidly—just as a sandcastle can be built with ease. However, every sandcastle is threatened by the rising tide, and our fear must be that the fabric of our society will lack the strength and resilience to cope with the growing crisis. The resilience we need is not only financial (which we manifestly lack) but also societal: the ability to nurture our children and care for the vulnerable and elderly. Likewise, we must fear that the psychological health of our nation will prove too fragile and will burden the state with ever more mental illness and chronic sickness, as well as antisocial behaviour, sexual promiscuity and the catastrophic costs associated with STDs and unwanted pregnancies. We must fear that the economy, having tipped from production and growth towards consumption and debt, will depend too exclusively on the financial and professional services sectors for recovery and growth—sectors that can provide employment for only a small proportion of the population. An economy so narrowly based is highly precarious in a global downturn. We must fear, too, that the political contract will break down and democracy will become little more than focus-group consultations and news management, offering scant leadership to make the longer-term and increasingly costly choices that now face the whole human race.

## *Study questions 3*

1. Why does the erosion of social foundations create greater social fragility?
2. In what ways have Western societies become fragile?
3. What psychological role does consumption now play in the 'developed' world?
4. What are some of the potential negatives of a wealthier population?

# FOUR

## Bowing the Knee: the Ascent of Money (PSC)

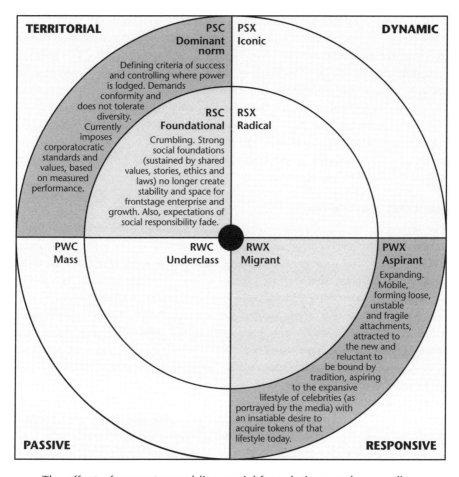

The effect of current crumbling social foundations and expanding aspirations in the West on the dominant norm

## Chapter summary

In this chapter, we explore the Dominant Norm sector of the social ecology model, which I have labelled 'PSC'. Every society has an image (explicit or not) of the ideal citizen, and this represents a 'norm' against which individuals can be measured. Everyone aspires to match this ideal, whether it is expressed in economic or ideological terms, and those who succeed in doing so are invested with power as a result. Those who are seen to have failed are disregarded, while everyone else continues to strive to attain the standards this dominant norm demands.

This element in society is *'presented'*, in that it is highly visible. It also exerts *strong* rather than weak force, in that its thrust is relentless, without regard for most of the forces that oppose it. Finally, it is also *'consolidating'*, rather than 'expanding', in that its effect will tend to be to resist both diversity and change as it imposes its singular vision of an ideal life.

The dominant norm applies in those areas of society that are governed by explicit, contractual agreement. So, for example, the law and the people who enforce it require standards of behaviour that citizens by and large consent to. However, there are also more informal, non-contractual ways in which such a norm is imposed—for example, the measurement of our society's wealth in terms of its 'gross domestic product', or GDP, is a PSC principle that, while generally accepted, has never been formally agreed.

## Summary statement

*The argument of this chapter is that, though historically the dominant norm in the West has covered a broad range of considerations, including conscience, social responsibility and good citizenship, today it is more and more narrow, being defined almost exclusively in terms of personal financial wealth. As a result, the institutions that have become powerful because they promote this norm are, increasingly, those that trade money, whereas those that promote other values (such as moral conscience, social responsibility and good citizenship) have been disempowered. A new, more constricted hegemony of commercial and financial power has slowly but steadily taken control of the mechanisms of political power and intruded into the way that every aspect of society functions. Consequently, the models of governance and management that are now used in what were once social and professional occupations, such as health care and education, are borrowed from the marketplace of private commerce. Equally, values of competition and individual acquisition have displaced other values such as consideration, creativity and the common good.*

........................................................

The tools you need for the beach, to build your sandcastle, are buckets and spades. There is little in life that gives more instant gratification than packing a bucket with damp sand, turning it over, giving it a couple of pats and then lifting it off to reveal a perfectly moulded tower underneath!

Of course, the only way to keep your sandcastle standing in the long term is to keep the bucket over it. If you can't build on foundations, you need to build inside a shell. Rather like an insect, which lacks an internal (or *endo-*) skeleton and instead supports and protects the soft parts of its body with an external (or *exo-*) skeleton, a sandcastle must be encased in something strong if it is to endure.

## *Government as the imposition of control*

It would hardly be surprising, therefore, if a society that had consistently undermined its own foundations and moreover had recklessly built with sand then found itself resorting more and more to dropping a bucket over its crumbling ramparts to restore their shape. The structure is essentially unstable and increasingly needs to be held together from the outside because it lacks internal cohesion. When this starts to happen in social systems, it becomes almost inevitable that some forms of control will have to be imposed.

The interventions of an ever more intrusive 'nanny state' have become the cause of increasingly loud complaints in Britain as people feel that the authorities are interfering in their private lives and taking away their civil liberties. New 'anti-terror' laws greatly extend the police's powers of arrest and restraint, and the courts can now restrict our freedom with 'anti-social behaviour orders'. CCTV cameras monitor our every move, while the roads are watched by ever more speed cameras, and we are being threatened with ID cards. These and other mechanisms of top-down social control are a response to anomie, the absence of those 'backstage' forces (such as respect for elders and for institutional and parental authority) that used to hold society together. They are inevitable, and may even be necessary, now that our communities have lost their self-discipline.

This application of strong state power on the front stage is akin to someone patting down their sandcastle with a spade to try to prevent it collapsing. Unsurprisingly, it is restricted less and less to the actually criminal or antisocial as the government treats every citizen with suspicion. Public services such as education, health and social services are increasing dominated by bureaucrats. In state education, a national curriculum is now dictated by civil servants in Whitehall. The freedom of teachers to be spontaneous, to follow their own instincts and go off at a tangent is now virtually eliminated.[33] Moreover, the targets now set by central government treat both the health and the education service like a factory assembly line. Units of production are counted, and quality is assessed against a set of national criteria with no local variation permitted. Penalties are imposed when productivity falls below the required measure and the results of regular inspections are made public for all to see.[34]

## Government as customer service

As the foundations of our Western societies have given way, so our sense of identity as responsible citizens has also disintegrated. We are no longer citizens enjoying the privileges of our social system, we are aspiring consumers. We judge our public services in the same way we judge Tesco or McDonalds. We see it as our right to demand all the treatments we want and expect the state to provide them for us. In response, the government has increasingly over the past two decades tried to impose on the public sector the mentality of private-sector industry. It has applied the same measures of performance to its healthcare providers that the private sector applies to a factory or to a company listed on the stock market. For economic reasons, it has sought to manage the public sector like a private enterprise, and indeed has privatized much of it, from our coal mines and steel foundries to our buses and trains, our prisons, our postal service and, increasingly, our hospitals—and soon our state schools as well. Patients and pupils alike are referred to as 'customers' or 'clients'. In a society in which people see themselves not as citizens but as consumers, the politicians who get elected are the ones who understand what the market wants and (promise to) deliver it.

The result is that we have allowed the flow of financial rather than social capital to dictate the shape of our civil society. This has happened in two ways. The first relates to government spending. In the private sector, there is an assumption that if you want better services you have to pay for them, and the government has bought into this and 'invested' huge amounts in (for example) our health service. This extra spending inflates the market, however: doctors' salaries soar, and so does the cost of equipment and resources, while only comparatively

---

[33] 'There is now a torrent of evidence emerging that Britain's rigid, centralised approach to teaching has utterly failed in what it set out to do. ... Teachers had lost much of their autonomy and discretion, and were frequently obliged to follow pre-prescribed lesson plans laid down by Whitehall, rather than engaging with the children in front of them': Jenni Russell, 'The NUT Has Cried Wolf Too Often, But This Time It's Right', *The Guardian*, 26 March 2008, p29

[34] 'Since the first Conservative management "reforms" on the NHS in 1973–4, a bewildering number of procedures that derive from commercial models of management have been relentlessly demanded by both political parties within a system that is quintessentially professional (non-commercial) in its outlook and ethos': Professor Paul Brown, unpublished article, 2006

modest gains have been achieved in terms of patient waiting-times, for example. Nonetheless, the government is able to point to its investment strategy, as well to incentivize the health-care providers to reduce patient-doctor time and rack up greater productivity. Health care is transformed from a professional, public service into a private industry, assessed against the same financial benchmarks. Thus, the second way in which we have allowed capital flows to shape our society is that the culture of the national health system (for example) has become that of the private market, where performance is judged by a set of criteria that are ultimately all financial, concerned with reducing costs, maximizing revenue and hitting productivity targets rather than improving patient well-being and the quality of care. It is, after all, much easier to measure progress in monetary terms.

## Government by the market

In this way, as a nation, we in Britain have found ourselves being governed by the rules of the market in areas that were previously the domain of social responsibility. And this highlights the fundamental shift in our social ecology, which has destabilized the delicate balance between freedom and responsibility. We have changed the 'social game' we play from one about citizenship and participation into one about the market and consumption. The ultimate object of any civilised society must always be the well-being of its members and their safe, meaningful, creative, energetic and peaceable interaction. However, since the end of the Second World War, this overriding purpose has increasingly been supplanted by another: the generation and management of financial capital.

The economy as a system of markets is a derivative of a social system—a mechanism for trading goods and services. It is not an end in itself. It serves an end, which is the well-being of people within that system. The benefits it offers include employment and the chance to improve their lot for those who are fit to work and welfare for those who are not, and opportunity for those who are creative and entrepreneurial. As long as the economy serves that greater end of human flourishing, it can function appropriately. However, over the last few decades we have seen a subtle but hugely significant change in our social discourse that indicates that it no longer serves the common interest but rather subordinates it.

Listen to any report on the health of our or any other country and the measure that is generally used is GDP. This expresses the size of the economy, being the sum of the financial transactions that occur in a year within its boundaries. It takes into consideration only how much is sold and bought and at what price. It takes no account of what goods are used for, for example, or of how wealth is distributed through the population. GDP could grow and yet the gap between rich and poor could widen. It could grow and yet 90 per cent of the population could get poorer. It could grow and yet the happiness, security and mutual trust within the population could diminish. GDP is now regarded as the basis of social health in the West and accepted without question as its proper measure, even though (as the Greens point out) by this measure an ecological disaster counts as a positive because it boosts economic activity. Recession—dread word!—is no more than the contraction rather than continuing expansion of an economy, and yet it is regarded as an object of terror, which governments must prevent at all costs, the cause of all kinds of evil, from rising unemployment to falling pensions.

## *Human life becomes less human*

What this represents is the domination of financial capital that we have come to accept as axiomatic in how we value ourselves as a society. There are four implications that flow from this change. The first is a dehumanized vision for human life. The moment we start to value people in terms of how much they earn, we begin to see them as mere utilities. It is dismaying to see how we now identify celebrity almost exclusively with financial wealth—not that all rich people are famous, but that everyone who aspires to be famous does so because they believe it will make them rich. As a society, the people we put on pedestals tend to be those with financial assets. It is a national disgrace that we hold activities such as academic research and teaching in such low esteem that we seem to be content with a market that pays a footballer in a couple of weeks as much as such public servants, who are building the intellectual and social capital of the next generation, may earn in a year.[35] Moreover, we have convinced ourselves that we are getting richer as a nation because our GDP has grown so massively over the last two decades, and there is increased investment in education and ever more technological advances—regardless of the fact that in other terms, such as social cohesion, trust, happiness and security, we have seen either no progress at all or an actual regression. In fact, research suggests that average levels of individual happiness in Britain have not risen one inch in the last 20 years,[36] while we have witnessed the continuing disintegration of our communities and family structures.

---

[35] The starting salary for teachers in London was £25,000 in 2008, according to the Association of Teachers and Lecturers (retrieved on 2 April 2008 from http://*www.tda.gov.uk/recruit/ becomingateacher/startingsalary.aspx*). The average basic salary of a footballer in the English Premiership in 2006 was £676,000 a year, or £13,000 a week, according to a survey of professional players by the *Independent* published in that paper on 11 April 2006.

[36] 'Happiness pundits cite the lack of any connection over time between recorded levels of happiness and material wealth (GDP), both in the UK and across the developed world. GDP in the UK has

## The emergence of the 'corporatocracy'

The second implication is that we have created a new master to toil under: a 'corporatocracy'. In a democracy power is (in theory, at least) distributed across the population, but in a corporatocracy it resides with neither the people nor the leaders they elect but an uneasy coalition of government and industry, whose interests become conflated. For example, it is no secret that America's post-war foreign policy involved forming alliances with countries across the Middle East (such as Egypt, Saudi Arabia and Iran), the Far East and Latin America (such as Ecuador, Panama and Colombia), which involved 'helping' them to develop their economies.[37] Typically, American energy consultants advised the governments of these countries on how to assess and plan for the construction of the infrastructure they needed in order to exploit their natural mineral resources, and the governments then borrowed from the World Bank the huge sums of money required.[38] Many commentators have criticized the cosy relationship between the Washington-based World Bank, Wall Street and the American Treasury. The debts that were run up were so vast they were virtually impossible to repay. Usually, these governments awarded the construction contracts to one or more of America's massive firms, which ensured that the capital they'd borrowed flowed back into America's economy, and to its Treasury. Moreover, sometimes America took a controlling stake in their state-owned industries, or else it took advantage of their indebtedness at a later date, perhaps by requiring them to vote a certain way at the United Nations or to allow its armed forces to use their territory or airspace. Politics, finance and big business were fused into a single axis of self-sustaining power.

## The gap between rich and poor widens

Such a strategy ensured that America attained an unprecedented position in the world, in terms of both political dominance and control of resources and industry. It also meant that globally financial capital flowed from the poor to the rich. We are always told that the justification for the capitalist system is that, however unequally the 'cake' is divided, nonetheless capitalism makes it bigger and so everyone gets a larger slice. However, the evidence suggests that the opposite is true. This is the third implication of the domination of financial

---

doubled since 1973 yet ... happiness has hardly changed at all': Paul Ormerod, 'Sorry, You Won't Find Happiness This Way', *The Sunday Times*, 8 April 2007, p4

[37] Robert A Rosenbaum, *The Penguin Encyclopedia of American History* (Penguin Books, 2003), p128

[38] *Confessions of an Economic Hit Man* (Berrett-Koehler Publishers, 2004) offers one account of such dealings from the personal experience of one American agent, John Perkins.

capital. Ultimately, it has not closed the gap between the haves and the have-nots but has actually widened it. This is the case not only in America but also in many of the 'developing' countries it has 'helped'. Sadly, the effect of loans from the World Bank has often been to line the pockets of corrupt politicians in majority-world countries while the rest of the money flows straight back into Western bank accounts.[39]

## Rising global aspirations jeopardize sustainability

Fourthly and finally, the domination of financial capital makes it very difficult for the world to respond to challenges that require any kind of multinational co-operation that involves a reduction in GDP growth. The aspirations of the 'developing' world are focused on catching up with the levels of wealth and consumption enjoyed by the 'developed' world. India and China's new middle classes aspire to the lifestyles of their European and American counterparts—and what right do we have to deny them the opportunity? However, the reality is that such equality, even if it could be attained, could never be sustained—the planet simply does not have the resources to allow it. Indeed, unless the West itself changes course, it will be responsible for leading the rest of the world into very perilous waters.

## Challenging the notions of ownership

If the fundamental problem is the domination of financial capital, the solution must lie in the subordination of that capital to other measures of wealth and health. This can be achieved only if our understanding of ownership is changed. Many large businesses are now talking about 'the triple bottom line', which recognizes profit or loss in environmental and social as well as financial terms. This kind of language is an attempt to bring into the valuation of profit-making business some other criteria than purely financial profit. However, as commentators have pointed out, while it is very easy to draw up a balance sheet to gauge a firm's financial performance, it is far more difficult to measure the 'social profit' or 'environmental costs' it has generated. How much should a sexual harassment lawsuit be worth, for example? What value should be attached to more just terms of employment for factory workers in the Philippines? The measures become too slippery, too vague and too subjective to be useful and may only allow companies to claim they are taking responsibility for their impact when actually they are not.

---

[39] Nick Cohen, 'When Giving to the Poorest Just Lines the Pockets of the Richest', *The Observer*, 17 September 2006, p11

The alternative is to accept that we have a perfectly good system for putting a financial value on things and we are best to stick with that. What needs to happen is that a larger constituency of people owns shares in each publicly listed firm than is currently the case. In the new terminology that is now gaining currency, 'stakeholders' would need to become shareholders. We all broadly accept the idea that suppliers and customers are to some extent 'stakeholders' in a business, but we have not gone so far as to recognize that their 'stake' should actually constitute a 'share'. Until this is the case, the notion of a stakeholder is a con that counts for nothing. There are a few models of business ownership based on such principles that look promising, and we shall examine them in the second half of this book.

These, then, are the four implications of the domination of financial capital:

- a dehumanized vision for human life that ultimately reduces people to commodities fulfilling a commercial function
- the emergence of a new structure of power: a corporatocracy which is neither elected by nor accountable to the people, which conflates the interests of government and big business
- a growing imbalance in the distribution of wealth
- a lack of any real means to make financially costly decisions internationally

Like a bucket over the top of a sandcastle, financial capital has dictated the shape of the post-war global economy. The 'hard' measures of financial value have subordinated all other, 'softer' measures of social value and environmental impact. The unregulated global free market advocated by Milton Friedman has prevailed as the only viable system, and has been accorded its own moral authority. Political decisions are now determined by the rules of the market alone. A financial 'mould' can be pressed onto every element of social life—be it health, education, the arts...—to impose the same shape upon it, and this uniformity gives governments an easy measure to assert and assess their targets for improvement and justify their policies and budgets. Our social system has changed from one that is built from the bottom up on the concrete of moral consensus, social responsibility and political participation to one that is formed and held together by the impositions of an unelected but increasingly powerful alliance between politicians and businesspeople, who may have scant regard for their social, environmental or moral impact. Commerce shapes society and imposes its values on citizens, and in allowing this we have allowed ourselves to become merely consumers, defined by our purchases.

And besides the 'buckets' that determine our values and direct our spending, our fragile, aspiring populations must increasingly be 'patted down' by the force of laws and regulations and the threat of the penalties attached to them. We no longer internalize our social boundaries as psychological norms and so increasingly they are imposed as legal constraints. Inevitably, society is ever more monitored and restricted and the police are given more and more powers to curb antisocial behaviour. The nanny is given the tools to keep her charges in check.

## Study questions 4

1. When the foundations of a society are eroded, what sort of top-down control tends to be exerted in their place?
2. What role does the market now play in controlling politics in the West?
3. How has the social contract between citizens and the state been altered in the West over the last 30 years?
4. Is there any alternative to either the public or the private ownership of business (and therefore capital)?

# FIVE

## Buying the World Cheap (RWX)

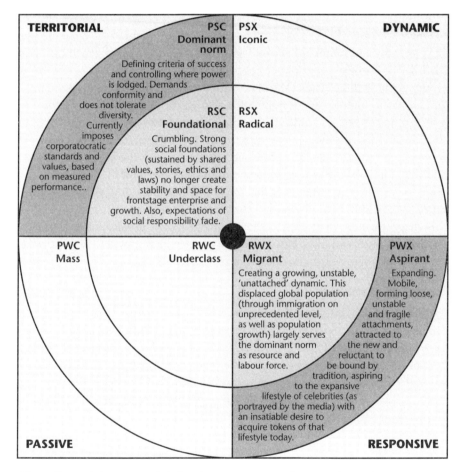

The effect of the powerful dominant norm on the growing migrant sector

## Chapter summary

In this chapter, we explore the Migrant sector of the social ecology model. I have labelled this 'RWX', and it is the reaction within the system to the action of the PSC dominant norm. It is *'reserved'* as opposed to 'presented' because it is largely hidden beneath the surface of society. If the PSC represents what people aspire to, the RWX represents that which the PSC sector controls.

The force this sector exerts is weak rather than strong in that those within it have migrated in response to opportunities that are created by powerful economic systems elsewhere. They do not themselves create the market, but they do serve it. And the sector is *'expanding'* in that the Migrant population literally moves to where the opportunities arise. This is what migration involves: breaking free of your roots and removing yourself and your dependants to a new location in the hope of finding work or safety or whatever.

Combine these three characteristics together—reserved, weak and expanding—and we have a highly reactive population that serves the needs of those who are powerful in our society. Indeed, we might observe that the PSC sector creates the market opportunities and structures that the RWX sector then reacts to and serves. The former tends to dictate the terms on which the latter can operate, and this obliges the RWX sector to be highly flexible, mobile, responsive and available. At the same time, it is the *'hidden'* sector, providing support, service relied on by, but out of view of, the 'front stage' buyer. The argument of this chapter will be that, even as the dominant norms in Western society have become stronger and more controlling, so the need has grown for a responsive, 'migrant' population to service those normative PSC expectations.

## Summary statement

*The growing financial power of the PSC corporatocracy has meant that the legitimate broader social needs and rights of those from whom it buys goods or services are increasingly overlooked. The imbalance of power means that traditional forms of trade have become intolerably inequitable. Politically, the RWX population is an uncomfortable fact that many governments would prefer to deny. Economically, it represents the less affluent and therefore less influential members of society. Physically, it often lives in areas that are hidden away, quasi-ghettoes or enclaves where ethnic minorities become concentrated, rather isolated from the surrounding neighbourhoods. There may be long-term consequences of the social disruption their migration causes that have yet to be addressed.*

Is there limitless sand? On holiday last year on the south coast of England, I observed several major operations in progress as beaches whose sand had over time been washed away were replenished by the local authorities. Trucks would dump their loads in huge piles at one end of the beach, and diggers and earth-movers would then spread the sand across, covering the eroded areas and building them up against the action of the sea. Presumably, there was another beach somewhere that had a surfeit of sand and could happily spare it. Strictly speaking, no sand is ever lost, it is merely moved from one location to another. Perhaps that movement is global and the little patch of beach I was watching on the south coast of England once lay under the palm trees in Borneo. Who knows?

## *Borrowing to buy sand*

In much the same way, the 'sand' from which our society has built its metaphorical castles has all come from somewhere else. One feature of globalization is the ability to transport goods around the world. Supply chains grow ever longer. One region of the planet, the West, lacks enough raw materials to go on building but can buy them from elsewhere. In 2007, America (for example) had borrowed nearly $700 billion against its national bond in order to continue this redistribution.[40] It had a monthly running trade deficit of $64 billion, of which 20 was with China alone.[41] At the same time, the British treasury had run up a record debt in relation to overall GDP.[42] Moreover, at £1.4 trillion, consumer debt in Britain had reached unprecedented levels. The availability of credit with minimal down payments had become an endemic problem for Western society.

I wrote this chapter originally in 2007, but since then the world has changed. What has happened has exposed the utter absurdity and irresponsibility of the consumptive borrowing that has sustained global economic growth for the past 15 years. It has become clear that the entire global financial system

---

[40] US House of Representatives Committee on the Budget, 24 July 2007 (http://budget.house. gov/doc-library/2007/foreignhelddebt_hearingsummary.pdf)

[41] 'Remarks by Treasury Secretary Henry M Paulson, Jr. before the Economic Club of Washington', US Treasury press release, 1 March 2007. Retrieved on 2 April 2008 from http://www.treas.gov/ press/releases/hp285.htm

[42] 'Provisional estimates show that for the calendar year 2007 the UK recorded a government deficit 43.8 per cent of GDP': 'UK Government Debt and Deficit', National Statistics (2008) (http://www.statistics.gov.uk/cci/nugget.asp?id=277). This represents an increase on previous years, according to 'Euro-indicators', a press release from Eurostat dated 17 August 2007: 'Reported data ... show ... a government debt to GDP ratio of 42.5% in 2006/2007 compared with 41.6% in the previous year' (http://64.233.183.104/search?q=cache:qAhY1BMlVhUJ:epp. eurostat.ec.europa.eu/pls/portal/docs/page/pgp_prd_cat_prerel/pge_cat_prerel_year_2007/ pge_cat_prerel_).

was built on a parcelling-out of bad debt in ways that were fundamentally unsecuritized. The collapse of the financial markets represents nothing more than the inevitable (and entirely predictable) results of consuming more than the world can sustain and, in effect, fabricating money as a means to negotiate the trade of real commodities. It makes little difference whether we are talking about borrowing in relation to retail spending, or spending on real estate, or government spending on services and capital building projects: the financial markets had evolved to allow unprecedented levels of expenditure, in order to maintain unsustainable levels of acquisition, both personal and public. We may blame the bankers, but arguably the real culprits are the politicians who based their electoral mandates on increasing their country's GDP (and the tax revenues that went with it)—GDP that, in effect, consists of nothing. Their guilt is only underlined by their eagerness to reinflate their shrinking economies with yet more borrowing. Their addiction to inflated tax revenues has driven them to inject yet more poison into the system, the toxin of 'buy now, pay later', encouraging the public, too, to go on buying and consuming insatiably.

Of course, this trade in goods has been fuelling tremendous growth in Asian and other economies; but how long can it go on? What social consequences are those countries suffering that are supplying the demands of the West? And how stable are those demands? From the perspective of the suppliers, there are some basic questions to be asked about the relationship in terms of power and control.

## *The growth of the migrant class*

The growth in the Asian 'tiger' economies has largely been balanced by a decline in the corresponding sectors in the West, mainly in manufacturing industry and agriculture, which have been replaced by low-level service industries. The coal mines of Nottinghamshire and the steel works of Glasgow have closed, and the employment they used to provide must now be sought in the range of low-level service industries that serve the dominant brands that feed our consumption of goods: construction companies, call centres, supermarkets and superstores. One thing these have in common is the flexibility of their working hours. However, working '24/7/365' means that people become divorced from the rhythms of wider society. Moreover, employment contracts are typically short-term and temporary, allowing employers to assemble a flexible labour force to which they are less committed. The result is a kind of migrant working class, detached from their local communities and at the beck and call of their corporate masters.

## Squeezing the supply chains

However, it is not only their employees who are in servitude to corporate masters: their suppliers are under relentless pressure to reduce supply costs. The fair-trade movement may represent an ethical protest against the exploitation of the labouring class around the world, but global free markets mean that every supplier has to cut his costs if he is to compete—otherwise, the purchaser can simply buy coffee from Colombia instead of Kenya, their bauxite from Jamaica instead of Australia. One of my Indian students from Bangalore tells me that his friends are giving up their careers as engineers, health workers or teachers because they can get better pay working in the call centres of a Western bank. The threat to his country is very great: talent and training are lost and vital professions are deprived. The stability of the economy is being undermined—and, moreover, it is becoming vulnerable to the same forces that brought it the bank's custom in the first place. What will happen when it is cheaper to relocate the call centre to Indonesia or Brazil?

## *What price unrenewable resources?*

It is not only people who are exploited as a global commodity: so are the resources of the planet. The fierce competition in the global market and the pressures corporations can apply drive down the price of goods as well as encouraging unethical practice and the despoliation of the environment. Illegal logging in the Amazon Basin, for example, feeds the insatiable demand for hardwood garden furniture in Britain, while great swathes of rainforest are burnt down so that cattle can be grazed or soya grown to supply the Western market—even though the thin Amazonian soil will support them for no more than a few years before it is exhausted. In the 1970s, there were dire warnings about the growth of the global population and the planet's limited ability to produce food. Those fears have proved to be unfounded, so it seems, because we have developed more intensive farming techniques—and yet there is now not one agricultural region of the earth where the soil is not seriously depleted or eroded and unable to sustain the yield we now expect from it.[43] Water, too, is a growing problem—for example, in the rice-growing bowl of India, where wells have been sunk ever deeper (often financed with Western aid) in order to irrigate the land as modern agriculture demands. In many regions, the aquifers

---

[43] Matleena Kniivila, 'Land Degradation and Land Use/Cover Data Sources', working document from the Department of Economic and Social Affairs' statistics division dated 31 December 2004 (http://unstats.un.org/unsd/environment/envpdf/landdatafinal.pdf); Keith Wiebe, 'Will Land Degradation Prove Malthus Right After All?', *Amber Waves*, June 2003 (http://www.ers.usda.gov/amberwaves/june03/pdf/awjune2003resources&environmentfinding2.pdf)

these wells tap into have already sunk from six metres to 150 metres below the surface.[44] Australia's recent drought was a result of the excessive demands made on its principal rivers—a catastrophe for one of the world's breadbaskets.

What is an acceptable cost to a country to supply the demands of the developed West? The loss of talent? The loss of control? The loss of social cohesion? It would seem that the risks involved in the deal are overwhelmingly borne by the supplier and not the buyer, and their partnership is very unequal. Power is not distributed equitably, or even humanely. Once again, it comes down to a question of ownership. Is it right that suppliers should have no share in the firms they supply? Is it right that consumers should have no obligations to those who produce the goods they consume?

## *Mass urbanization*

One consequence of all this is increasing migration from the countryside to the city, to create ever larger metropolises, where vast factories can produce goods at lower cost through economies of scale. The displacement of communities in the majority world is a result both of voluntary migration and eviction. Plans to dam major rivers, whether to generate electricity or to deal with some problem in water supply, require the removal of whole communities to burgeoning urban sprawls. In China, for example, the government is rehousing huge numbers of people in distant cities to make way for massive dams.[45] It is estimated that as many as 15 million farmers will lose their land in the years ahead, and already riots have broken out over compensation. In Europe, meanwhile, national and urban infrastructures are struggling to cope with the integration of large immigrant communities, not least from Eastern Europe. The ability of a country to absorb outsiders in a healthy way, which breeds goodwill rather than suspicion and gives people opportunities for growth and social mobility rather than trapping them to run-down ghettoes, depends not

---

[44] 'In Tamil Nadu, a state with more than 62 million people in southern India, wells are going dry almost everywhere. According to Kuppannan Palanisami of Tamil Nadu Agricultural University, falling water tables have dried up 95 percent of the wells owned by small farmers, reducing the irrigated area in the state by half over the last decade. As water tables fall, well drillers are using modified oil-drilling technology to reach water, going as deep as 1,000 meters in some locations. In communities where underground water sources have dried up entirely, all agriculture is rain-fed and drinking water is trucked in': Lester Brown, 'Aquifer depletion' in The Encyclopedia of Earth, 12 February 2007. Retrieved on 2 April 2008 from http://www.eoearth.org/article/aquifer_depletion

[45] 'Nowhere have the costs of dam-building been more visible than at China's Three Gorges, the world's largest—and perhaps most notorious—hydropower project. Begun in 1994, the dam forced the migration of millions and led to high unemployment in the region, deadly landslides, pollution and other environmental problems': Andrew Batson, 'Rising Tide: Dissent Slows China's Drive for Massive Dam Projects', *Wall Street Journal* (Eastern edition), 19 December 2007 (http://online.wsj.com/article/SB119802214926737977.html?mod=googlenews_wsj)

on its luck or (primarily) the national temperament but on its social capital. Inevitably, migration and displacement fracture the bonds of the social ecology in those host communities. Families lose their sense of attachment to land and place, exchanging it for a shiny new life hundreds of miles away. The benefits of established social structures are traded for a few white goods. The change is inevitable, but it poses all kinds of questions for societies as the stories and ties that have traditionally held them together are replaced by something new.

## *Mass migration*

Migration within countries mirrors migration from the 'developing' to the 'developed' world. In Britain, we have recently been experiencing an influx of immigrants from Eastern Europe. Since the EU expanded to include a number of these former Eastern Bloc states on 1 May 2004, an estimated 585,000 people have migrated to Britain from this part of the world.[46] Government estimates had put the number at around 13,000. In 2007, incomers to Britain totalled about one million. This is immigration on an unprecedented scale, which looks set to increase the population of this country by 20 per cent by 2050. Often, these migrant workers have several, very low-paid jobs, as builders, labourers, cleaners, waiters, nannies, au pairs, fruit-pickers or farmhands. Go into any bar in London and, as like as not, you'll find it staffed and maintained by Poles and Romanians. The availability of so much cheap labour has kept costs down and some analysts estimate that without it interest rates in Britain would be 0.5 per cent higher. It is clear that the Government regards economic migration as an expedient way to prevent the economy from stagnating.

However, throughout the 'developed' world, such populations of migrant workers are vulnerable and easily exploited. They do not enjoy all the same rights as the citizens of their adopted countries and can expect low wages and poor working conditions where their health and safety are inadequately protected. It is difficult for them to protest against their treatment and face the continual pressure that others will replace them if they are unhappy with their work. Moreover, alongside so much legal immigration, there is now the global problem of illegal immigration. In America, the border with Mexico is now a place of danger, policed not only by state guards but also by vigilante groups trying to stem the flow of illegal immigrants. Estimates put the number of illegal immigrants in America at over 11 million[47]—who, again, offer cheap, easily exploited labour that boosts the economy.

---

[46] 'Migration: Net Immigration 191,000', National Statistics (2007) (originally found at http://www.statistics.gov.uk/cci/nugget.asp?id=260)

[47] 'In summary, there were an estimated 11.6 million unauthorized immigrants living in the United States as of January 2006. Nearly 4.2 million had entered in 2000 or later. An estimated 6.6 million

In Europe, the points of entry from Africa and Asia are similarly policed. Thousands of people are encamped on the coast of Morocco hoping to make a desperate crossing to Gibraltar or Spain just a few tantalizing miles away. The scale of human trafficking is immense, and the fate of the people who are 'imported' in this way is often appalling. The drowning in 2006 of 21 Chinese cockle-pickers who were working for a Chinese gangmaster on the coast of northern England drew attention to the virtual slavery in which many illegal immigrants live. Meanwhile, many vulnerable girls and young women who agree to be smuggled into Britain or other affluent countries in the belief that well-paid jobs await them end up trapped in prostitution.

In part, this flow of migrants is a result of the flow of capital from the countryside to the cities and from the 'developing' to the 'developed' world. In part, it is caused by the wars all over the world that are making huge numbers of people homeless. In part, it is a consequence of our continuing failure to address the deep problems of Africa in particular. The outcome, in any event, is instability and lack of cohesion.

## *Exploiting the desperate*

Desperation energizes anyone, man, woman or child. The deeper you dig down through Abraham Maslow's hierarchy of needs, the more primal the sources of energy you find. In all of us, the drive to survive is strong, and although our experience of prosperity in the West may have made us apathetic, those in the majority world who lack it hunger for it. Uprooted from their places of origin, they live as temporary aliens in a foreign land. They have no sense of connection or belonging to the places where they now live and work, which lack the traditions of home for them. They have lost their sense of identity. The desire to be 'at home' runs deep in all of us: we crave a place where we can settle and feel safe and establish a relationship with our environment. Human communities have always made up stories and traditions about the places they live in so as to give them a shared sense of identity, belonging and history. When people groups are displaced, as refugees or exiles, they lose these 'psycho-geographical' attachments and markers. They become vulnerable and unsettled—easy to exploit, easy to influence but hard to predict. Globally, migrants are a volatile population, disempowered and yet energetic, without any proper place or voice and yet craving for their lot to be improved.

---

of the 11.6 million unauthorized residents were from Mexico': Michael Hoefer, Nancy Rytina and Christopher Campbell, 'Estimates of the Unauthorized Immigrant Population Residing in the United States: January 2006', *Population Estimates*, August 2007, p1. Retrieved on 3 April 2008 from http://www.dhs.gov/xlibrary/assets/statistics/publications/ill_pe_2006.pdf

It is worth noting that it is often such social conditions that result in revolution. In the end, slaves so resent their slavery that they seek to overthrow their masters. It is only a matter of time before the cauldron of anger and desire and the energy they generate can no longer be contained by the social 'lid' that is put on it and that anger, desire and energy start to boil over. What ensues will be spontaneous and chaotic, impossible to predict and extremely hard to manage or contain. Ultimately, it is futile to try to make the lid tighter or more secure. The only way to subdue the volatility is to improve the circumstances that have caused it in the first place. As long as their circumstances drive them to desperation, people will resort to desperate—and even suicidal—measures. Only when they believe they have something worth preserving will they begin to show a proper concern for their own safety, prompted by a proper sense of dignity. The current policies of America and Britain in response to the global threat of Islamist terror are catastrophically flawed, in that they are designed simply to contain the contents of the cauldron while the West continues with the strategies of political and economic domination that lit the fire under it in the first place. As long as we persist with those strategies, the resistance will still bubble away—and unless we turn the heat down, sooner or later it will boil over. It's basic physics, and basic social ecology. Let's hope there is no explosion.

## *Study questions 5*

1. What is the link between the dominance of the corporatocracy and increasing migration?
2. Who is in control in this situation?
3. What are the dangers for economies built on a migrant class?
4. What are the long-term implications of long-term migration for a country's social capital?

# SIX

# Celluloid Slavery: the Economics of the Celebrity Class (PSX)

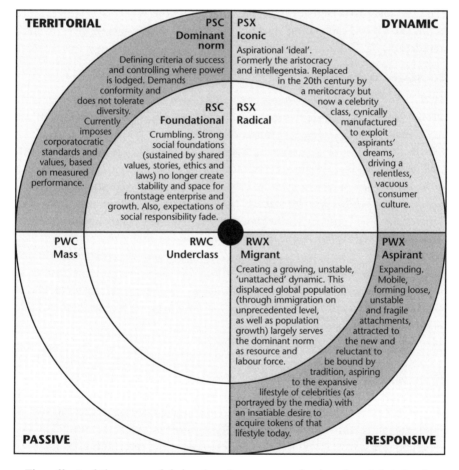

The effect of the powerful dominant norm on who has 'iconic' status in the West today

## Chapter summary

In this chapter, we explore the Iconic sector of the social ecology model, which I have labelled 'PSX'.

This element in society is, obviously, highly visible, and so is *'presented'* rather than 'reserved'. It exerts a *'strong'* (as opposed to weak) influence over the direction that others will take—not least, the Aspirant sector of society, who tend to imitate the iconic classes. It determines the fashions and styles and influences the values to which we aspire. It is also *'expanding'*, in that it takes us into new territory: the novel, the exotic, the exhilarating, the risky. That is its appeal—the glamour of it all!

Put together, these three characteristics—presented, strong and expanding (PSX)—define that element in society that lights the way to a brighter, more confident future, captivating those who follow it and inducing them to look and dream.

## Summary statement

*In this chapter I will argue that over the last century the nature of what is iconic in our society has changed dramatically. Historically, it used to consist of the social elite, the so-called upper classes. The 20th century saw a gradual shift to a meritocracy, in which we looked up instead to people who, through some virtue, skill or effort, had accomplished something out of the ordinary. However, recently a further shift has occurred whereby we now admire people who have little, or even no, discernible talent or achievement. The label 'celebrity' fits this new aristocracy better than 'icon', and an individual can win it almost regardless of any merit. This chapter will explore how and why this change has occurred, and the function celebrities have in our social ecology. I will maintain that the creation of this new aristocracy is neither accidental nor surprising, but rather represents the extreme of the control exercised by the PSC dominant norm. The consequences of allowing our icons to be manufactured to reflect such values back to us are profoundly damaging to the well-being of our society.*

In my family, building sandcastles is always a competitive business. At some stage in any day on the beach, one of us will throw down the gauntlet to the others. It doesn't really matter what the challenge is, as long as there is one: to build the tallest, the widest, the strongest, the most intricate, the most lifelike—or simply the one that will last the longest against the returning tide. Then we all set to, and for 40 minutes or so nothing can be heard but the sound of happy hands scraping, piling and patting sand.

There is something instinctive, and even atavistic, in the human desire to compete. Few societies have emerged that have not offered some kind of prize for the best fighters or runners or riders or wrestlers. We seem to have a basic need to push ourselves to our limits, and an urge, too, to identify those in our society who have performed supremely well. We honour them with titles and medals and reward them with money, prestige and even adulation. The desire to build the best sandcastle on a blustery day on the English coast is just one small expression of a universal urge that drives human endeavour at the highest social, industrial and economic levels around the world.

And it leads to the creation of the social elite.

## The reconstruction of the iconic class

Every society has its elite, who determine the horizons and the aspirations of the rest. In Britain at the start of the 20th century, this would have included royalty, the nobility and the gentry, who lived a life apart in terms of wealth, power, status and culture. As their titles were inherited, they created dynasties. It was in these 'upper-class' circles that fashions were dictated—in clothing, pastimes, decor, education and travel. The social elite was also associated with pushing back the intellectual and political frontiers. It is no coincidence that in Britain both the Fascist party and wartime traitorous spies emerged from within the ranks of the nobility. Of course, political and military power rested disproportionately with the aristocracy.

A hundred years ago, our society revered the wealthy, landed elite. It revered the intelligentsia. It revered its political and military leaders. It deferred to them, accepted their authority and followed their ideological lead. However, over the course of the past century we have gradually transferred this esteem to others. Tragic failures of leadership perhaps contributed to this development, not least in the First World War. Up to that time, all army officers were drawn from the gentry, regardless of ability, and they commanded such little respect that it was not uncommon for their men to shoot them in the back when they were ordered to advance from the trenches. In response to this, after 1918 the British Army became the first institution to develop psychological tests so that it could recruit officers who had genuine leadership skills rather than mere breeding. This was a significant move towards meritocracy. At the same time, the growing availability of education to the wider population gradually disseminated social, political and intellectual power from the elite to the 'lower' classes. By the 1960s, the intellectual agenda itself was to denounce the hegemony of the wealthy 'upper' classes and deconstruct the traditional and institutional forms of power in our social system. The iconic influence of the aristocracy was fast being eroded.

## *The role of the media*

Who replaced the aristocracy in our social ecology in the role of social icons? A key factor in the rise of a new breed was the influence of the media. The media provided the means whereby the attention of the whole population could be directed towards particular individuals—by the broadcast not only of words (for example, in radio talks given by the members of the elite) but also of images. The celluloid celebrity was born. The shift from an essentially verbal culture to a visual one marked the end of a culture based on thoughts and ideas. Ideas cannot really be conveyed successfully high profile through images: they can be illustrated, they can be animated and made more compelling, but they always rely in the end on the logic of words, the sense of the sentence. The visual as the basic media form upon which the second half of the 20th century was to be built ensured that ultimately our icons would be visual, sensual and aesthetic in nature.

Unimaginable wealth now flows into the hands of those who the public wants to look at. In 1992, the average salary of a soccer player in the Premier League was £75,000.[48] Compared with the incomes of most other people, that was substantial but not exorbitant. Nowadays, such a player would be earning on average more than £1 million a year, as a result of the huge television audience (not least on subscription TV) and the very high prices people will pay to go to a game.[49] A similar story can be told of stars in both the film and the music industry. Tom Cruise earned $75 million from *Mission Impossible*. Madonna is reckoned to have grossed over $260 million from her single 2006 tour, in addition to all her other revenues that year.[50]

The fame and attention such icons enjoy is no less extraordinary. They can be assured that they will be invited to every premiere, every gala, every party that matters. Moreover, their endorsement of clothing or other branded goods will earn them enormous fees. We will wear what they wear, get our hair cut like theirs; we will buy the magazines that offer them to us. The influence some of them have appears to be limitless. Where the world's politicians and diplomats have failed, they can get debate going within the G8 about lowering trade

---

[48] 'In 1992–93 the average wage for a Premiership player was £75,000 per year. In 2001–02 the average wage for a Premiership player was £600,000': Vivek Chaudhary, 'Forty Factors Fuelling Football Inflation', *The Guardian*, 31 July 2003 (http://football.guardian.co.uk/comment/story/0,9753,1009392,00.html)

[49] 'On average, the league's players each earn more than £1m a year; a top player like Liverpool's Fernando Torres can cost £20m or more': Theo Leggett, 'Foreign Owners Boost UK Football', BBC News, 9 August 2007 (http://news.bbc.co.uk/1/hi/business/6938866.stm)

[50] 'Paramount: Cruise is Risky Business', CNN, 23 August 2006
(http://money.cnn.com/2006/08/22/news/newsmakers/cruise_paramount/index.htm);
http://www.billboard.com/bbcom/yearend/2006/touring/top_tours.jsp)

barriers, cancelling international debt and increasing aid to the majority world. Bono and Bob Geldof command more attention on the global stage than all but the most senior of the world's political leaders. When they champion a cause, the world listens.

## The role of the celebrity

However, there is a trade they make with the public in return for such wealth and influence, and that is their lives. They sell us themselves, their appearance and their persona. They become publicly owned goods and as such must dance to the tune the public demands. Of course this must be the case: in the economy of this market, what such people provide is more than simply an image of glamour, style and beauty, it is availability. As we observed in Chapter 3, what the aspirant population lacks is emotional rootedness—and it looks for this, and for meaning and identity, through celebrities. The celebrity industry first and foremost provides a social avenue for identifying yourself in society, but in addition it provides an emotional avenue for understanding yourself. We demand not only availability from our celebrities but also intimacy, as we crave to know all about their inner lives, their messy stories and secrets. We demand those paparazzi shots of Jennifer Aniston or Britney Spears emerging from their apartments, baggy-eyed and bed-haired, to pop down to the gym. We long to see what they look like behind the mask. We have a desire to feel emotionally connected with them. In this way, we see our own imperfections and insecurities mirrored back to us. We discover, ultimately, that we are not alone in the universe and someone else shares our mess. In the absence of a family in which we can find a sense of self, intimacy and belonging, we reach out to the remote-but-intimate celebrity. They become our emotional comforter, reassuring us when we feel lost. They show us a life we can only dream of, perhaps, but they also console us in the life we actually live.

## The role of the 'puppeteer'

People have always been inspired by heroes and heroines. It is essential for the health of a nation that its people aspire to the qualities of men and women of remarkable character or achievement, who excel in their courage, compassion, energy, skill or artistry. However, danger arises when such role models no longer promote values that are good for society as a whole. In the corporatocracy of the West, the worth of our idols is defined increasingly not by their character or achievement but by their commercial leverage. Behind every 'star' is a promoter—whose eyes are fixed on the bottom line. The dark secret of our celebrity culture concerns not the public or the performer but those who manage the show. The fact is that the whole structure has been built and maintained by people from another part of the social ecology, in order to extract vast sums of money from desperate aspirants. Celebrities are celebrities only because the media pay them attention, and the media pay them attention only because it is profitable to do so. And that profit comes from two streams of revenue: direct sales of media products and advertising. Sky Sports will pay clubs multi–million-pound fees for the exclusive right to televise Premier League soccer because it can sell the broadcasts to its subscribers for an enormous profit. Manchester United and others will happily sign such a deal because it ensures that they can make huge profits from the sale of club merchandise to their now global audience.

When Real Madrid bought David Beckham from Manchester United in 2003, it did so less for the sake of his footballing prowess than because it wanted to break into the market in the Far East, where Beckham already had a huge following in China and Japan. The thinking behind the transaction came from the club's accountants, who were interested in only one thing: increasing its share value on the stock market. The star player himself was merely a commodity, a utility expedient for their purposes of generating greater financial power and reward.

The cultivation of celebrity has been a collusion between brand manufacturers, the media, aspirant consumers and the celebrities themselves, to create a circle of consumption and desire. In this transaction, the flow of financial capital runs from the aspirant consumer to the brand manufacturer, the media, the celebrity and, of course, the financial services that supply the loans on which the purchases are made. In return for their money, the aspirant consumer gets a sense of emotional intimacy and surrogate social identity, which makes up for their lack of any authentic emotional and social attachments.

## The role of the non-celebrity

The final twist in the tale of celebrity is the emergence of the non-celebrity. For the last decade, it has been a running joke that the quality of today's 'celebs' has plummeted. It's often said that you used to need to have achieved something in order to be famous but nowadays you need to be famous in order to achieve anything. The causality seems to have changed. Indeed, this is what you would expect: if the celebrity is merely the cipher of the brand/media conflation, their actual quality becomes increasingly unimportant. We pay attention to them simply because we are made to pay attention to them, not because they have any merit that commands our attention. Celebrity shows present us with a succession of 'C-', 'D-', and 'E-list' nonentities.

Consider the ironic story of Chantelle in the British version of *Celebrity Big Brother* in 2005. The usual very minor celebs were planted in the Big Brother house to be scrutinized for a few weeks—but included in their number was an ordinary young woman from Essex who had no celebrity 'credentials' whatsoever. The production company behind the programme called her 'Chantelle' and gave her a cover story about being a member of a girl band. As no one in the house had heard of any of the other 'celebrity' contestants anyway, no one twigged that they were being set up. And, of course, she won the contest, having similarly fooled the viewers. Since then, she has, in her own words, been 'living the dream', with TV appearances, fashion shoots and the whole media circus making her the celebrity she never was. Obviously, the media's motivation is to make money, which means they must be selling something to someone. But who is actually buying Chantelle when she really does have nothing to offer—and we know it?

The answer is: 16 per cent of Britain's teenagers for a start, who (according to a survey in 2006) believe they will find success as a celebrity. The odds against making the big time through a show such as *Big Brother* are, in fact, about 30 million to one, yet the same poll found that one in 10 of the teenagers surveyed would be willing to give up their education to appear on TV.[51] Here is the rub. A hundred years ago, the iconic PSX sector of our society was an all but closed group that outsiders could not aspire to join except perhaps through marriage. Since then, the terms of membership of the social elite have changed: from being inherited to being earned by merit to being won today by anyone who has the good luck to flash her body or land in bed while the cameras are rolling. The truth is that the non-celebrity is the most cynical of all media/brand creations. Whether or not Chantelle has qualities lacking in millions of other young British women—many of them lost and emotionally dysfunctional, all craving attention and looking for an identity, all aspiring to escape their present lives, all believing the dream that money and publicity would give them fulfilment—it now appears that they need no expertise, no discipline, no effort to make it into our social elite. Instead, they can get there, with a bit of luck, just as she did—as long as the cameras keep rolling and the audience remains interested. In the meantime, all they can do is to prepare themselves for the call: watching the right shows, buying the right products, drinking the right drinks, frittering their lives away without ever taking responsibility for their choices. And in the end they can

---

[51] 'Fame hungry teenagers are planning to ditch education and live in dreamland. More than one in 10 (11 per cent) young people would drop out of education or training to be on TV, according to new research from the Learning and Skills Council (LSC). And more than one in six (16 per cent) young people believe that they will actually become famous. However, the odds of being picked for a *Big Brother* style reality TV show and being successful afterwards are around one in 30 million': LSC press release 336 (2006), 'Kids Seeking Reality TV Fame instead of Exam Passes' (http://readingroom.lsc.gov.uk/lsc/2006/externalrelations/press/kids-seeking-reality-tv-fame.pdf)

assuage their inevitable disappointment by acquiring things that at least remind them of Chantelle's glittering Essex palace: the HD plasma screens, the white leather suite, the satellite TV, the holidays, the boyfriends.

And the cash they will need for these acquisitions? Well, there's always another credit card deal, always another six-month interest-free balance-transfer offer, always another way to pay off their debt in the future—and with only a £1 downpayment who can refuse? Meanwhile, the corporatocrats driving the machine press the buttons and pull the levers, create the brands and exploit the celebrities, finance the loans and squeeze the supply chains around the globe to manufacture the products, pocket the money and add another property to their portfolio of country residences.

Nobody builds yet another sandcastle unless they want to. The fuel of economic growth is discontent with what we already have. Capital expansion depends on aspiration. Encourage one and you encourage the other. And one of the key ways in which aspiration has been encouraged in the West has been through the cynical manufacture of a new 'celebrity' class. Crucially, members of this class are valued primarily not for their skills but for their potential financial leverage—that is, how effectively they and whatever brands they endorse can be sold. This has been a key means corporations have used to enlarge their markets. However, in the process they have created social icons who are not admired, let alone held to account, for their values and principles. Those who idolize celebrities and seek to emulate their lifestyle therefore adopt ideals and aspirations that are at best socially neutral and at worst socially damaging. The net impact of this new aristocracy on our society is to have encouraged aspirant consumers to aspire to wealth and fame (or, indeed, notoriety) rather than more noble attainments that require self-discipline, self-sacrifice and commitment as well as good manners. As a result, the dreams of the rising generation are being squandered and the vital energy that is needed to sustain a vibrant, creative, fertile and mature civilization may be waning.

## Study questions 6

1. How has the composition of the ruling classes in the West changed in the past century?
2. What is the psychological function of the new celebrity class?
3. Who is controlling it and profiting from it?
4. What is the social legacy of this situation?

# SEVEN

# The Rending of Our Social Fabric (PWC)

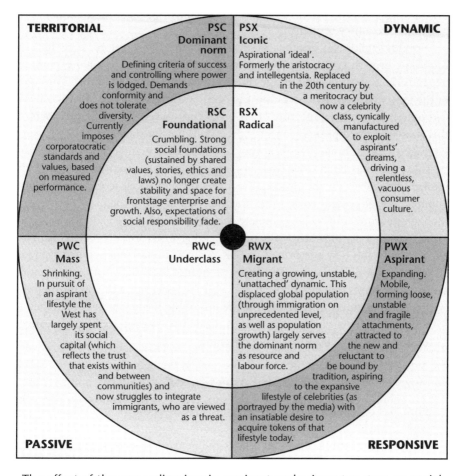

The effect of the expanding iconic, aspirant and migrant sectors on social capital in the West

**Chapter summary**

In this chapter, we explore the Mass sector of the social ecology model. By this (which I have labelled 'PWC') I mean that which gives cohesion to any social system.

This element in society is visible, and so is *'presented'*, but the force it exerts is weak in that, by and large, the bonds that hold society together consist of trust, respect, compassion, social proximity, shared interest, a shared heritage and so on, rather than contract and obligation in any legal or economic sense. This effect of this element in a society is to consolidate it rather than expand it. It creates cohesion rather than mobility; it represents the roots people put down rather than the acquisitions they take with them. It is fostered by shared stories, community events, festivals, traditions and local practices and customs—all those things that bind people together at a subliminal level.

**Summary statement**

*This chapter will argue that in most societies people belong to wider collective groups: families, clubs, teams, communities and so on to which they have some kind of attachment. The strength of such bonds has been diminishing over the past 50 years. As a result, our society has been losing its resilience, as well as its ability to foster talent. Moreover, the social roles people used to play informally, such as policing their neighbourhoods and protecting the vulnerable, now have to be carried out formally and contractually by the state, which will increasingly place an unsustainable financial burden on the economy.*

......................................................

There is sand that is great for building castles with and sand that, despite all your efforts, just won't do the job. The ideal sand for building is neither too fine nor too coarse. Too fine and it gets cloggy and sticks to the bottom of the bucket; too coarse and it lacks coherence and behaves like mere grit. However, the most crucial ingredient in a good sandcastle is the right amount of moisture. You want to be working with sand that was under water a few hours before: not saturated, but not dried out by the sun, either. If the sand is too dry, it is best to have a partner who can bring water back from the sea to wet the sand so you can work with it.

## *The essential function of social capital*

What is it that gives the 'grains' of society coherence? What binds individuals together to form a cohesive community? The magic ingredient is the glue of social capital. Like financial or intellectual capital, this is an asset or form of wealth that can be exploited. Some of this capital is 'spent' when 'costs' are incurred in absorbing outsiders, for example. If a society has enough in the bank, as it were, it can generally afford to pay the costs of integration—and there always are costs. However, if its bank balance is low, it may quickly run into the red. Unlike financial or intellectual capital, you cannot amass social capital by selling or buying things. It cannot be grown through a government programme. It cannot be borrowed, or multiplied through the markets and strategic investments. Nor is it the preserve of an institution, organization, government, company or any other collective body that can own it. And for this reason it is both more fragile and more precious than other kinds of capital.

At its simplest, social capital is the trust that exists between people. This is what makes it unownable. It is a commodity that is present in the space between human beings: between one human being and another, between individuals in a community and between communities; between the elderly and the young, between the rich and the poor. Social capital is the bonds that hold the social fabric together, the transactions that bind the social ecology into a stable whole. If financial capital is the monetary wealth of a society and intellectual capital the wealth of ideas that it possesses and can exploit, then social capital is the wealth of trust it can rely on. It is the richness of the spaces between people, the unpaid-for, invisible ties. It is the soil of society in which each individual plant grows. Social capital therefore consists in the closeness, integrity and reliability of relationships in any community.

## *Nurturing potential*

A society rich in social capital can do a number of things. First, it is able to cultivate, direct and mentor talent. Small, local, family-run businesses act like a net to catch the potential of the rising generation. When 16-year-olds leave school and don't go on into further education, they need to find employment; and such a society can channel this stream of potential informally into useful occupations. When I worked in the East End of London, it was expected that a young man would learn his father's trade, or another relation's, and end up in his workshop or office. Uncles took on nephews in the family building firm and trained them on the job, or often there was someone in the extended family who owned a garage, who would take an apprentice. In this way, young men (in particular) who had no future in white-collar professions were able to find a place in society and a way to make a living.

## Self-policing

Second, such a society can police itself. In close-knit communities, the behaviour of any individual youth is always seen by someone else who knows their mum or dad or an aunt or uncle. A neighbour of ours has lived in this part of our city most of her life, as have her mother and her children and grandchildren. Mary knows most people locally simply because she has been around; she is connected to almost everything that goes on. One day, she was on a bus when two youths began swearing and abusing other passengers. She marched straight up to them and said: 'Right, I know who you are. Let me tell you that I know your uncle and if I see you carrying on this kind of behaviour, you'll have him to deal with.' Of course, their misconduct stopped there and then. It is not just ordinary people who are connected: there is also the network of local public servants, from the bus conductors to the park keepers to the refuse collectors to the local postmen and women who, simply by being around and being familiar with people, prevent society from becoming anonymous and unaccountable.

## Caring for the vulnerable

Third, a society rich in social capital is able to care for the elderly and the vulnerable in its midst. In 2003, France discovered how depleted its social capital was when a drought caused the deaths of some 15,000 elderly people across the country, and in Paris especially. Many died in their own homes, unremarked. No one knew these old folk were there; no one visited them.[52] They were not members of church congregations or lunch clubs or voluntary organizations that would have noticed their absence. They were, in effect, invisible. Much the same could be said of the population of New Orleans, similarly left to their fate in the wake of Hurricane Katrina. Here in Britain I recall one local doctor telling me that when she prescribed a course of treatment to an elderly or vulnerable person, she would ask them whether they had any relatives nearby. If they did, she knew they had a much better chance of completing the course of treatment, as she would ring the relative and ask them to visit her patient regularly to check that they were taking their medicine. Social capital underpins a society's ability to care for its elderly and vulnerable members at an informal level, through the exercise of compassion, goodwill, generosity and 'other-person-centeredness'. It reflects the extent to which each member of that society looks beyond their own individual life, or that of their nuclear family, and feels a sense of responsibility for others around them.

---

[52] 'Paris Continues to Feel the Heat from a Deadly Summer', Jo Johnson, *The Financial Times*, 24 December 2003, p6

## *Welcoming incomers*

Fourth, such a society is able to befriend outsiders. Both Britain and America have strong traditions of welcoming immigrants in the belief that their societies will be enriched by their cultural and economic contributions, and as a result both countries are richly multiracial and multicultural. However, in both cases the relationship between the host culture and those of the immigrants has not always been easy. Distrust can easily build if it is seen that newcomers are receiving preferential treatment (in terms of housing, for example)—which is often the case when immigrants have larger families than other people locally—as well as taking jobs and helping to drive down wages. Usually, it is the perception of socio-economic injustice that lies at the root of ethnic tension in urban areas rather than race per se. Broadly speaking, though, in both Britain and America the social integration of people of other races has been possible because of a set of values and practices shared by the host nation: toleration of expressions of faith and ideology other than your own, confidence in your own national identity, a clearly defined set of social conventions and norms, festivals and rhythms that enable immigrant communities to understand and participate in the host culture, a market which incomers can enter and where they can prosper on the same basis as anyone else if they work hard, and, finally, an interest in the rich and colourful cultural diversity that is expressed on the 'front stage' of that society as a result.

## *Raising the next generation*

Fifth, such a society is able to nurture healthy, well-adjusted children. Crucial to the development of emotional stability in any individual are sound relationships with primary caregivers who are consistent in imposing their values and norms. In such conditions, children grow up learning to trust both themselves and other people. They also learn social responsibility within the context of the family as they witness the effect of their behaviour on those around them and see themselves within a wider set of relationships. Families also provide the context for intergenerational learning, as experience, tradition and wisdom are passed on over the meal table or while walking the dog or sharing a story at bedtime. The young learn to appreciate the contribution of the old, and the nature of vulnerability. They learn to see themselves within a historical tapestry of society and are exposed in a healthy way to the realities of both birth and death. Moreover, institutions such as the churches and historic faith-based organizations can help children and adults alike to develop a sense of the sacred and of the rhythms of the year, and to exercise the disciplines of self-restraint and thankfulness, generosity and compassion. All this can have a profoundly humanizing effect on our emotional and social formation.

The web of relationships we are talking about—with families, local small businesses, schools and congregations, neighbours and doctors and other public servants—form the very fabric of any society. None of these relationships are established purely by contract. These are not bonds between employers and employees, masters and servants—they are what we call 'weak' social bonds that rely upon trust and respect rather than financial or legal obligation. Even the marriage contract is based less on legal commitment than on the promises of the individuals concerned. The strength of such relationships lies in the ties between people and their willingness to help one another out.

When this pattern of relationships is widespread, society is healthy and stable and functions well. When it is not, other kinds of power tend to be exerted, which are either less accountable or more formal and dominating. Post-Soviet Russia is an example of a society afflicted in this way. Power and wealth there are concentrated in the hands of a tiny minority of the population. Access to the market is available only to a few. Power is exercised either negligently or oppressively by the state. Levels of alcoholism and other addictions are rising catastrophically, and many observers are predicting an associated Aids crisis in the years to come, as the bulk of the people become relegated from the 'front stage' of their society, where they had status, purpose, opportunity and hope, to its 'back stage', where they languish as an underclass. Any society that is poor in social capital will similarly be seriously weakened. Essentially, it is able to do far less to help itself than a society that is rich in social capital, as each of the capacities we have discussed above are undermined or diminished.

## *The loss of social capital*

When we examine the evidence, we begin to see that one of the consequences of the growth of our financial capital and the subsequent domination of Western societies by monetary wealth has been a catastrophic loss of our social capital. The social bonds that in the middle of the 20th century were strong have since been seriously eroded. As a result, first of all, we are failing to nurture potential. There are fewer trades open to young adults, fewer small local businesses, fewer apprenticeships. In their stead, they may have to find employment in temporary shift work stacking shelves or staffing call centres, where young men in particular will not gain any sense of identity and self-respect. Moreover, the links between each generation of men and the next are weakened, as the old hands no longer act as mentors to the novices. The wisdom of experience is not passed down but instead leaks out of the system and goes to waste. Given that 80 per cent of crime in Britain is committed by disaffected young men aged between 18 and 25,[53] this is a serious problem.

Second, we are less able to police ourselves. Whereas in 1959 a British poll found that 60 per cent of respondents said that basically they trusted other people, by 2005 that percentage had fallen amongst younger people by over a third.[54] There may be good reason for this, of course. Crime—whether it be mugging, burglary or murder—is increasingly related to drug use, and criminals under the influence, who cannot to be reasoned with, are chaotic as well as lawless. We learn that the use of knives is rising, and hear too many stories of responsible citizens stepping in to prevent violence and only getting stabbed and killed themselves—and it discourages us from either trusting or caring for others. Moreover, as we break up our families and communities, we all become more anonymous and less accountable. Incidents such as Mary's intervention on the bus become rarer, and in some parts of our cities people do not dare to venture out after dark for fear of the gangs that roam the streets. My wife works as a behavioural adviser in schools, helping them to deal with dysfunctional adolescents, and she witnesses the problems first-hand. So often the means that are needed to constrain behaviour are simply not available. Fathers are absent. Parents are suspicious and angry and themselves offer violence to staff. Children who are excluded from school simply go out on the streets—while their schools employ bouncers to keep them out. It is a bizarre and tragic indictment that in a First World country with an economy of the size of Britain's some children cannot enjoy even basic safety at school, let alone an education.

Third, our ability to care for the elderly and the vulnerable has gradually diminished. Instead of this care taking place in the community, it has to be provided increasingly by the state. Today, 30 per cent of people who go to see a doctor in Britain do so in connection with psychological problems: depression, anxiety, loneliness and stress.[55] Perhaps it is no coincidence that, at the same time, recruiting for voluntary organizations such as the Scouts and the Guides has never been more difficult.[56] Meanwhile, instead of getting support through local clubs, associations, churches or the like, isolated individuals are increasingly

---

[53] 'Crime: 4 in 5 Offenders are Male', National Statistics, 8 January 2004. Retrieved on 27 March 2008 from http://www.statistics.gov.uk/cci/nugget.asp?id=442

[54] Paul Haezewindt, 'Investing in Each Other and the Community: the Role of Social Capital', *Social Trends* 33, National Statistics (2003). Retrieved on 6 April 2008 from http://www.statistics.gov.uk/articles/social_trends/socialtrends33article.pdf

[55] Undated survey of GPs conducted for Mind (originally found at http://www.mind.org.uk/Information/gpsurvey.htm)

[56] 'The age of philanthropic volunteering is gone. We need to produce things of interest and benefit to volunteers to make us appear an enticing opportunity': Simon Carter, head of communications and marketing at the Scout Association, quoted in 'Finding the Need', NCVO (n.d.), (https://www.ncvo-vol.org.uk/?template=1&template=1&id=2417)

having to turn to formal agencies, in the private or public sector, to meet their basic social needs. More often than not, my local doctor cannot rely on a local network or extended family to support a patient. Instead, he has to get in paid help in the form of home nursing funded by the state. The loss of social capital always results in more expense for the state, which has to step in as a surrogate to prevent people slipping down into an underclass.

Fourth, we are less and less able to welcome outsiders, but instead perceive them as threats. The open borders of both Britain and America are fast being closed, and tolerance is becoming a thing of the past. In part, this is a consequence of the devastating psychological impact of '9/11', which has made Americans feel vulnerable on their own soil and suspicious of others. The growing popularity of the re-emergent far right in mainland Europe demonstrates that this less open, less trusting and more defensive perspective on society is not limited to Britain and America. Part of the problem is the erosion of the shared values that give cohesion to our own cultures, into which we hope to integrate newcomers. Ironically, in our efforts to make room in our society for other cultures, we have damaged the very features that made our society attractive to them in the first place. Britain's liberal tolerance is rooted in a particular set of values, and you will find no such tolerance in Saudi Arabia or Afghanistan, which lack the same ideology of human life. Those values are fostered by and expressed in not only our secularism but also our spiritual traditions, which are unavoidably Christian. Our laws, which seek to protect the weak and offer asylum to refugees, which guarantee the rights of others and a fair trial, are all specific to our culture and history. They cannot be sustained without that context and that narrative—they do not exist in a vacuum. When we discard the religious basis of the festivals of Christmas and Easter, for example, so as not to discriminate against ethnic minorities of other faiths, we do them no favours. We are in danger of undermining the very things for which they came here.

Fifth, we are making the next generation increasingly dysfunctional. The proportion of marriages in Britain that end in divorce will soon reach one in two. At least one in two people has been affected in some way by a fractured home, whether as a child or as an adult—and everyone learns to parent from their own experience of being parented. More deeply, the formation of our own emotional well-being and sense of self and the development of our ability to trust others are related directly to our experience of reliable, stable relationships with significant others. Like seeds growing in soil that is continually disturbed, children who endure emotional disruption suffer damage in their emotional and social formation.

## *The social price of liberal morality*

Of course, the impact of technology has also had a deleterious effect on children. The average time an American adolescent spends in front of a computer or game-console screen is 21 hours a week. The effect of this is to reduce the influence of both their parents and their peers on their socialization. Children learn social skills through social interaction—primarily, through playing in groups and teams. Isolated individuals, interacting with a screen for hours each day, do not learn these skills or acquire emotional literacy. Not only this, but the content of the programmes they watch is often negative. A recent study on the effect on teenagers of watching soap operas—not video nasties!—found that they reduced their patience, trust and goodwill towards others and encouraged aggression and intolerance.[57] TV shows, no less than action movies and computer games, often reduce human interaction to a level where problems are resolved through hostility and violence, or else the abdication of responsibility; and such are the attitudes and behaviours that children learn, internalize and are given permission to exhibit.

Considering that in 2005 the biggest-selling computer game in the teenage market was Grand Theft Auto,[58] in which drug lords rob and kill and pick up prostitutes, is it any wonder we are seeing a rise in aggressive, antisocial behaviour and a lack of self-restraint in our young people? One of the truths of our day that has been most thoroughly and damagingly suppressed in the name of the free market, tolerance and individual rights is that engaging with such negative images and roles does indeed have a damaging effect on the behaviour of those who play these games. Of course, without a shared moral framework within which to discuss the issue, we seem impotent to regulate the market that generates such material. Thus, we find that our children fall victim to the pernicious, amoral operations of a gaming world that aspires only to make money, as well as to the boundary-free world of the internet.

Trust, respect, compassion, a sense of responsibility and a sense of belonging that has nothing to do with contracts are the glue that holds any society together

---

[57] Alison Motluk, 'Blame It on the Box', *New Scientist*, 6 April 2002 (http://www.newscientist. com/article/mg17423372.200); 'Dr Aric Sigman, an associate fellow of the British Psychological Society and author of a book on children and television, said: "It is the greatest unacknowledged health threat of our time. … The key stages of development are language acquisition and social skills and if they're displaced at this time they may be irreplaceable." He added: "Television is isolating. Children end up spending years in front of a screen instead of speaking and socialising with real children. As a result, they don't learn how to get on with other people. At the same time, faster editing with colours, zooms and a constant stream of images has been linked to a lower attention span"': Steven Swinford, 'Kids Behaving Badly After Just Two Hours' TV', *The Sunday Times*, 30 September 2007, p21
[58] 'GTA: San Andreas Toasts Success', BBC News, 4 November 2005 (http://news.bbc.co.uk/1/ hi/technology/4404088.stm)

and enables it to absorb and integrate immigrants. The West is discovering that the sand it is building its castles with is losing all its cohesion. Why, we may ask, has there been such a catastrophic loss of our social capital? It turns out that we have paid even more for our consumer lifestyles than the price that was exacted at the checkout, and it is a social cost we have largely overlooked, or else have chosen to ignore. We may be dangerously in the red in financial terms, but we are so, too, in social terms. We have spent our social capital with no thought for the future, and only now may be starting to recognize the scale of the investment we have squandered.

## Study questions 7

1. Why is social capital so important to the well-being of any society?
2. What can a society rich in social capital do that a society poor in social capital can't?
3. What are the factors that have caused the loss of social capital in the West?
4. Who benefits commercially when a society is poor in social capital, and who pays?

# EIGHT

## The Swelling of the Underclass (RWC)

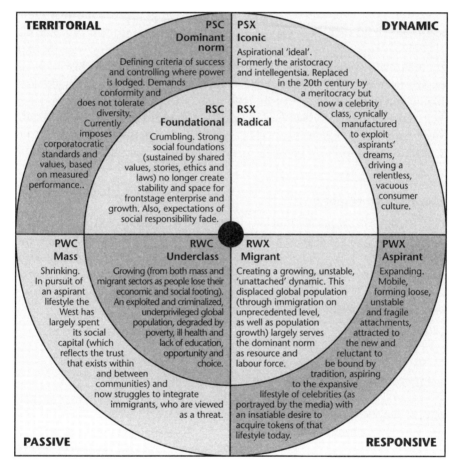

The causes and effects of a growing underclass

## Chapter summary

In this chapter, we explore the Underclass sector of the social ecology model, which I have labelled 'RWC'.

The underclass is typically *'reserved'*, in that most societies will try to hide this section of their population away. These people are, to some extent, its shame, or at the very least its awkward nuisance: the costly leftovers when their economic productivity has diminished. The power the underclass exercises is *'weak'*, in that it does not have political leverage or financial clout, educational privilege or career opportunities.

Moreover, it is *'consolidating'* rather than 'expanding' in the sense that these people are afraid that their world is being taken away from them and they try to cling on to it. They have lost the vision to make a positive contribution to society or to climb up the social ladder. In some ways, their behaviour is marked by despair. For some, as hope has died, so too have faith and goodness, dignity and self-control. For them, only a life of violence awaits. Others retain their sense of humanity but are so crushed in spirit they are unable to see beyond the task of surviving another day. They are characterized as RWC by their passivity, emptiness, impotence and vulnerability. Decisions are made for them by others.

## Summary statement

*The chapter will argue that in the social ecology model the RWC underclass represents the opposite of the PSX elite. The rise of the former parallels the rise of the latter. For a society to be healthy, its most powerful members need to show compassion to its most powerless, something that seems to happen less often today than in the past. There are more routes into poverty now than there have been since the advent of the modern welfare state, and there are fewer routes out.*

......................................................

As sand dries out, so its cohesion diminishes. Grains that previously were incorporated into a structure begin to separate and fall away. In a similar way, the underclass consists of people who have become detached and lost their place in the social structure and fallen away, no good to anyone.

Every society in history has had an underclass. This is that section of a population that lacks the economic, social or political power to choose. Such people have no opportunity to change their own future. They are essentially vulnerable and passive, dominated and dictated to, their fate decided by the actions of other social groups above them. Both isolated and crowded at the same time, they are impotent to influence the shape of the game, and soon become dispirited, lethargic, cynical and hopeless. In India, the so-called 'untouchables', who are supposed to be the lowest caste, are ignored, or else treated with contempt, by higher-caste society. Below them, however, there is yet another caste, the 'invisibles', who are so ashamed of themselves that they come out only at night so as not to be seen. Their role is to wash the clothes of the 'untouchables'. For Gandhi, the mere existence of the caste system and the injustice it represented was an appalling affront to his civilization. Other societies may not have such an explicit underclass as India, but they have them nonetheless: 'ghettoes filled with bums', 'the long-term unemployable', 'the mentally ill', 'the criminalized', 'the homeless', 'addicts and vagrants'. The names we call them may differ but the social reality is the same, and so is their place in the ecology of power, whether in Beijing or Berlin.

## Compassion and welfare: the pride of the West

There are two questions concerning the underclass in any society: What are the factors that put people there? And what measures are in place to prevent that happening—and, indeed, to enable those already there to escape? In Victorian Britain, life was grim for the underclass, and frequently short. The most vulnerable people in society—the young and the elderly and infirm—often ended up there, in the workhouse or the debtors' prison. Street children and those who were no longer able to support themselves and had no relatives to look after them were swept up and dumped in a convenient dustbin. Given the harsh realities of this past, the last hundred years of Western civilization have seen a remarkable shift in attitudes, with far more resources now available to those at the bottom of the pile. Great social revolutions such as (in various countries) the abolition of slavery, the universal provision of education and the introductions of a welfare system, a state pension and a public health service represent enormous advances which have prevented many people slipping into the underclass. The post-war years have been a golden age of social support in Britain, which has attracted many outsiders to this country to enjoy its benefits. There is no question that this generosity towards the underclass, expressed through both individual philanthropy and public provision, represents a high point in Western civilization. Indeed, there are those who argue that the health of any society can be measured in terms of its attitude to the weak and vulnerable—and on that basis we must celebrate the health of our own society.

## The growing global underclass

However, even as we acknowledge this, we may also question whether the same social compassion (not to mention political energy) still exists today to maintain that generosity. What is more, we understand better now than ever before that there is a link between the operations of the global economic system and the fate of those groups that end up at the bottom of the pile—and with greater knowledge comes greater responsibility. We also have to acknowledge that, while the underclass in our own, Western societies has benefited from their increased wealth, we now have a global economic system and so have to consider the global underclass within the same moral landscape as the domestic underclass. Both are intractable, because they belong to one global economy.

In the past, the factors that put people into the underclass were a mixture of birth, education, finance, health (or, rather, the lack of them) and, sometimes, war. These same factors operate today. If you are born in Sierra Leone or northern Uganda, you are born into a civil war. Not only your life but also those of your parents are under threat—not only from war but also from Aids, malnutrition, water-related diseases, even curable conditions for which your community lacks the cure. You have few educational opportunities, and they are precarious and may be destroyed by an enemy raid. You are surrounded by systemic corruption, which is part of your very culture. Work is scarce and the cattle your parents own could be lost if there is a drought. The mortality rate of under-fives in your country is 15 per cent. If you survive past the age of five, you may be abducted and forced to fight as a child soldier, to see and commit atrocities that might traumatize you for life.

If you are born in downtown Detroit, you may suffer from lack of nurture— maybe your mother never knew your father, who raped her and (while he was about it) infected her with Aids. Perhaps you are brought up by your grandmother, who hits you. Perhaps you drop out of school, along with your friends, and descend into gang life, drug use and crime. You could have your first stretch in prison at the age of 16 and learn there a way of life (or, at least, survival) from which you will see little chance of escape. You feel that you owe society nothing and society owes you nothing.

These two scenarios, which are so familiar to us, could be recast in different social contexts around the world, from Washington to Wellington. Some people, of course, slip into the underclass from the migrant sector. If, over time, the energy and drive that caused them to migrate in the first place fail—because their resources are exhausted, or their spirits are broken—they may sink into a passive resignation and despair. One wonders, for example, what will happen when the very large numbers of economic immigrants in Europe, grow old. Instead of boosting the economy, as they do at present, they will become an additional drain on the state's resources, requiring benefits, pensions, health care and so on. In exploiting the endless supply of imported cheap labour, the minority world is storing up serious trouble for itself in the future. There seems to be little long-term thinking behind current policy. And one can expand this observation to consider the future of migrant populations in the majority world. Moving from the countryside into megacities may fuel an economic boom for a decade, but the impact of 20 million human beings, crowded together but separated from their extended families, has yet to be seen. This is an unprecedented situation for humankind.

## The true cost of losing social capital

Furthermore, healthy societies have always relied to a great extent on their social capital to contain their underclass; but if that capital is reduced, more people—young, elderly, sick, unemployable—slip down, into the 'nether world' inhabited by the likes of Paris's invisible old people in 2003 and the poor of New Orleans in 2005. As I have argued above, in the absence of the informal social care provided by our social capital, the state has to take responsibility for policing, supporting and caring for the community. It is inevitable that, for both financial and logistical reasons, it is not going to be able to do so. Imagine how complex—and how unlikely to succeed—an intervention by the state would have been if my friend Mary had not been able to stop that antisocial behaviour on that bus! Someone would have had to call the police, and then perhaps there would have been a chase, an arrest, a prosecution, a trial, a community order overseen by the social services. The cost to the public purse would have been vast—and to what effect? Little good would be achieved, and it would generate resentment and hostility. Project that across the entire country and the task of trying to prevent people slipping into the underclass through the agencies of the state becomes simply unmanageable.

Likewise, the task of caring for an ageing population is becoming increasingly problematic. In the past, the elderly were cared for by their relatives, but our growing individualism and aspirant mobility have fragmented families and broken up local communities. They have also reduced the birth rate, which means that the working population is likely to shrink. Unless these trends are reversed and families again come together to care for their older members, the state will be faced with unsustainable costs. The effect of losing our social capital will ultimately be to decimate our financial capital. The purely economic arguments for rebuilding it are overwhelming.

## An unsustainable financial burden

If it is true that the underclass in the West is being swollen both by the dispirited migrant communities and as a result of the loss of our social capital, we are in trouble—for two reasons, one economic and the other to do with security. First, our society will not be able to afford the cost of care for all those who need it. Second, it will become increasingly difficult (as well as expensive) to police the global underclass, which is the primary source of the growing criminal population, dehumanized by a mix of cynicism, boredom, hopelessness and anger. Dealing with this population worldwide will be far costlier than addressing the causes. However, the really insurmountable obstacle to containing the global underclass is that it now wields an unconventional power of its own.

Ironically, the very technology that so often we have assumed to be accelerating our progress towards a more humane society is also enabling the forces of chaos to work towards its destruction. Mobile phone technology, for example, allows al-Qa'ida's loose network to coordinate its activities and to manage its funds. Technology is morally blind, and the opportunities the Web provides for invisible, untraceable flow of information helps a group of terrorists to operate just as much as it helps a group of social entrepreneurs. Already, it is clear that 'dirty bomb' technology is available 'out there', beyond the control of any single government. A global underclass that had access to such means of devastation and the desperation to use it could never be simply 'contained'.

The West has bought the world cheap. Ultimately, the problem of the global underclass is not a matter of too little aid or trade, or too much debt: it is a matter of too much consumption. It is impossible that wealth could become so concentrated in the hands of the shareholders of the multinationals with any other outcome. We have bought the world cheap and the price we have paid is not enough to sustain the dignity and hope of people who have sold almost everything they had. The poor may have always been with us, but now with a handful of 'box cutters' they can bring down the trade towers of the world.

## Study questions 8

1. Why is welfare the pride of the 'developed' world?
2. In your own society, who constitute the underclass and how does society deal with them?
3. In your opinion, is the world a more or less compassionate place than it was 20 years ago?
4. What are the financial implications of little social capital in relation to the underclass?

# NINE

# Death, Grief and the Changing Cycles (RSX)

| TERRITORIAL | | | DYNAMIC |
|---|---|---|---|
| | **PSC** Dominant norm | **PSX** Iconic | |
| | Defining criteria of success and controlling where power is lodged. Demands conformity and does not tolerate diversity. Currently imposes corporatocratic standards and values, based on measured performance. | Aspirational 'ideal'. Formerly the aristocracy and intellegentsia. Replaced in the 20th century by a meritocracy but now a celebrity class, cynically manufactured to exploit aspirants' dreams, driving a relentless, vacuous consumer culture. | |
| | **RSC** Foundational | **RSX** Radical | |
| | Crumbling. Strong social foundations (sustained by shared values, stories, ethics and laws) no longer create stability and space for frontstage enterprise and growth. Also, expectations of social responsibility fade. | Growing and inspirational. Possible source of new vision to fund social renewal. With Islam resurgent, the West is under pressure to formulate its own moral and spiritual footing again and develop an undefended vision of society. | |
| **PWC** Mass | **RWC** Underclass | **RWX** Migrant | **PWX** Aspirant |
| Shrinking. In pursuit of an aspirant lifestyle the West has largely spent its social capital (which reflects the trust that exists within and between communities) and now struggles to integrate immigrants, who are viewed as a threat. | Growing (from both mass and migrant sectors as people lose their economic and social footing). An exploited and criminalized, underprivileged global population, degraded by poverty, ill health and lack of education, opportunity and choice. | Creating a growing, unstable, 'unattached' global dynamic. This displaced global population (through immigration on unprecedented level, as well as population growth) largely serves the dominant norm as resource and labour force. | Expanding. Mobile, forming loose, unstable and fragile attachments, attracted to the new and reluctant to be bound by tradition, aspiring to the expansive lifestyle of celebrities (as portrayed by the media) with an insatiable desire to acquire tokens of that lifestyle today. |
| PASSIVE | | | RESPONSIVE |

A profile of the current distribution of the global population in the West using the model of social ecology

## Chapter summary

In this chapter, we explore the Radical sector of the social ecology model, which I have labelled 'RSX'.

This element in society is *'reserved'* because it acts subversively, working behind (and even against) the explicit ('presented') values of the system. It wields *'strong'* power in that, while it may not have institutional authority, it does have a compelling influence over the imaginations of the wider population. In a sense, it influences the direction of the future. And certainly it is *'expanding'* rather than 'consolidating': this element in society longs for change and seeks to bring it about. It believes in a new order that will be better than the present one.

## Summary statement

*This chapter will argue that Western society is coming to the end of an era that began with the Renaissance in the 15th century. A founding vision of human life that produced five centuries of cultural, intellectual and industrial productivity has been lost. In its place there is a profound absence of any compelling ideology of what it means to be fully human. There is an urgent need for the West to rediscover its own moral and spiritual roots, so that it can enjoy a new growth of cultural, intellectual and, arguably, spiritual life.*

..................................................

Most sandcastles do not last even a day. One of the pleasures of a visit to the seaside is to walk along the beach early in the morning when it has been washed clean and smooth by the tide. Perhaps a few rounded contours remain of the biggest ditches and ramparts of yesterday, but otherwise all sign of its labours have vanished. The sand is laid out again by nature pristine and ready for fresh acts of creation, fresh statements of defiance against the inevitable, with only the memory maybe of what stood there before to inspire today's builders.

Of course, most human civilizations have left traces that time has not yet erased, but the fact remains that civilizations, like sandcastles, inevitably fall. As the poet Shelley wrote of the imagined ruin of one ancient monument:

> *...On the pedestal these words appear:*
> *'My name is Ozymandias, king of kings:*
> *Look on my works, ye Mighty, and despair!'*
> *Nothing beside remains. Round the decay*
> *Of that colossal wreck, boundless and bare*
> *The lone and level sands stretch far away.*

Theorists of social history divide into two camps: there are those (such as Spengler and Sorokin) who see history as cyclical and those (such as Hegel and Marx) who see it as trend-based and evolutionary. There are many in the West today who retain the prevailing optimism of the 18th-century Enlightenment that the human race is, broadly speaking, launched on a trajectory of self-improvement and progress. Often, advances in technology are cited as evidence for this. Some point to advances in medicine (such as the discoveries of penicillin, anaesthetic and antiseptic), health (sanitation and water purification), agriculture (intensive farming and genetic modification), communication (the personal computer, the internet, the mobile phone) or education. However, it is a mistake to confuse advances in technology with advances in human well-being and civilization. Sometimes, indeed, a step forward in one area of our social ecology is countered by a step back in another. For example, the intensive farming methods developed since the 1970s have indeed sustained a global population explosion of nearly two billion, but arguably at an unsustainable cost to the quality of our agricultural land and the health of the water table. In parts of Africa, it has merely prolonged the habitation of otherwise uninhabitable desert margins through food aid given by the UN.

## The panacea of technology?

Instead of solving our problems, technology has often merely deferred them to the next generation. The discovery of nuclear fission made possible nuclear power, but also nuclear war (not to mention the dirty bombs I have referred to above). We now have the ability to kill more people at a single blow than any previous generation in history. The advent of the internet has opened the doors of knowledge, but has also made it easier for paedophiles to groom children and has arguably facilitated and accelerated both a new global traffic in human beings and informal, supranational terrorist networks. In fact, technological advances merely change the context for human behaviour. Technology is no more than a tool which can be used just as effectively by the murderer as by the doctor. The real measure of human progress is what we choose to do with it: whether humankind—worldwide, not just in the West—is more just, more fair, more humane and more compassionate than it was even a century ago. On this measure, the evidence is far more ambiguous.

## Revolution, not evolution

The model of social ecology suggests that human history follows neither an evolutionary nor a cyclical path, but instead describes an expanding and contracting spiral. Here we come to the final sector on the chart of our social ecology: RSX. The combination of these characteristics—'*reserved*', '*strong*' and '*expanding*'—suggests that this area of society will be source of visions, ideals and dreams that catalyse and energize the drive into the future.

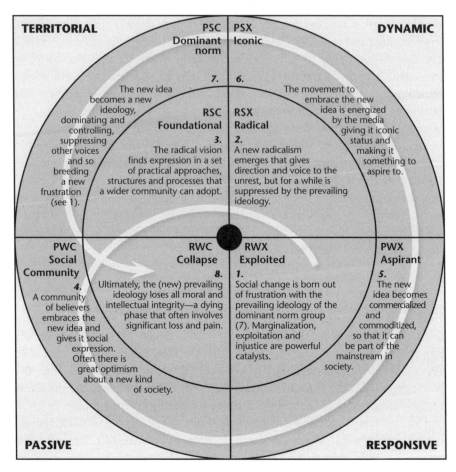

The model of social ecology applied to the general way in which social change takes place

This final sector of any social system marks both the beginning of the end and the end of the beginning: the death of the old and the birth of a new society. History never repeats itself exactly, never returns to quite the same point: the parameters change and different civilizations, cultures and populations become involved as the spiral turns. The spiral dynamic is shown in general principle in the diagram above.

# The end of the current cycle

If what I am saying is true, Western history seems to be coming to the end of the current cycle of its social ecology, which began properly with the Renaissance. Western manufacturing, facilitated by technological advances and fuelled by a religious ideology that encouraged people to work hard, save and invest, laid the foundations for the capitalist expansion of the succeeding two hundred years. It was the ideals and aspirations of that period, as well as its industry that provided the basis for the British Empire and the global dominance of first Europe and then America.

It is clear that the current financial crisis did not begin 12 months ago. Nor did it begin in 1986, with the so-called Big Bang in the City of London. Nor did it begin after the Great Depression of the 1930s. In fact, the real societal origins of the present crisis lie five centuries back. What we are witnessing today is the ending of an era that began in the 15th century with the Renaissance.

The diagram on page 80 charts this period of human history in terms of social ecology. It suggests that what we are now experiencing is the seventh of eight stages of social change: the collapse of the prevailing financial orthodoxy, which was established in a period of ultimately unsustainable industrialization, growth and consumption.

## Stages in Western cultural growth since the Renaissance

*Stage 1: Radical Renaissance (RSX, 15th Century).* An intellectual and cultural revival in Europe involves the welding together of Classical thought and Christian theology. The result is an explosion of cultural, intellectual and artistic creativity and exploration. Many of the finest examples of European architecture and art are produced in this period; the foundations of modern science are laid, and the intellectual scope of European thought is expanded to embrace science, philosophy, literature, art and commerce. This vision of a full human life, funded by a theistic view of the universe, propels Europe into its richest period of intellectual flourishing.

*Stage 2: Reformation Foundations (RSC, 16th Century).* This intellectual liberation leads to a shift in power from church to laity, and from church to state. In due course, the principles of 'the good life' are to become the foundations for political governance across Europe: notions of law, state and civic power, individual freedom and also commercial obligations. A Reformed theology full of gratitude for Christ's sacrifice and a strong sense that human beings are stewards of Creation produces the so-called Protestant work ethic, with its emphasis on hard work, duty and productivity, while belief in a better world to come—that is, heaven—encourages self-discipline, self-denial and investment in the future as key principles of the economy. The foundations for capitalism are laid.

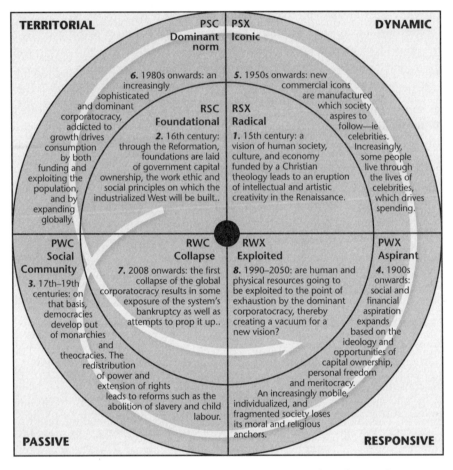

The model of social ecology applied to Western cultural growth since the Renaissance

*Stage 3: Social Equality and Democracy (PWC, 17th–19th Centuries).* The shift of power from church to state is paralleled by a shift from a single ruler to collective rule. Monarchies topple. The establishing of democratic forms of government across Europe is built on the theological belief in the inherent, equal value of every human individual. Democracy fulfils three intellectual convictions: to preserve individual freedoms, protect the vulnerable and prevent tyrannical abuse of power. The political outworking of the theology of the past two centuries leads further to radical reforms in education and health care and the abolition of the slave trade, child labour and, in due course, racial inequality. At the same time, people start to forget the RSX theistic world view that funded all these developments.

*Stage 4: Aspiration (PWX, 1900s onwards).* Increased personal freedom and better access to education produce a meritocracy. Aspiration funded by the Protestant work ethic, liberated by social meritocracy, accelerated by educational opportunities, driven by a belief in the goodness of progress brings in a hundred years of acquisition and consumption. However, the theological and moral anchors of the RSX world view have by now been lost. Progress is seen as something good in its own right, rather than as a preparation for another, heavenly life, and is understood in entirely materialistic terms. The RSC sense of moral obligation to state, neighbour and spouse is weakened as it comes to be regarded as intellectually indefensible; the RSC moral foundations of society collapse, leading to psychological dysfunction and social fracture.

*Stage 5: Iconic (PSX, 1950s onwards).* A new iconography, no longer religious but commercial, further fuels aspiration. Devotion to the new icons—celebrities—results in unprecedented growth in spending as people try to acquire the same lifestyle. A new psycho-spiritual orthodoxy based on consumption develops in the second half of the century, in which brands, like new traditions, provide identity and meaning in an ideologically empty society. Brand-makers use increasingly sophisticated means to manufacture consumer hunger through advertising and product placement.

*Stage 6: Dominant Orthodoxy (PSC, 1980s).* The consumptive orthodoxy is funded by an increasingly sophisticated mechanism of markets and finance. This makes possible unprecedented levels of capital lending, leading to an explosion of consumer and commercial debt. Increasingly, politicians define well-being in purely financial terms (GDP) and predicate their manifestos on economic growth. This in turn liberates corporate taxes to fund public spending, resulting in an insatiable corporatocratic monster that needs to feed itself with spending, debt and taxation. Addicted to spending and unable to define well-being in broader terms, governments irresponsibly promote consumer spending, leading to unsustainable levels of debt.

*Stage 7: Collapse (RWC, 2008).* The first collapse occurs. The corporatocracy inevitably begins to consume its own innards, borrowing from itself and inducing its own collapse. This is sharp and brutal but not, at this stage, necessarily final. Governments rally to prop up the system by nationalizing banks and pumping money back into the system. The final collapse may be deferred for a later generation to deal with as countries sink ever deeper into debt and, in the West, manufacturing industry continues to decline. It remains to be seen whether our addiction to consumption itself will, or can, be addressed.

*Stage 8: Exploitation (RWX, 1990–2050?).* Consumption relies on the increasing worldwide exploitation of raw materials. People migrate around the world into massive conurbations as human resources are redeployed to feed the appetite of global industry. However, the unrenewability of mineral resources, as well as the ever-growing global population, means that this appetite can never be satisfied, and the breakdown of the system is only deferred to some point in the future.

The pain of the current collapse is acute. It is a bereavement, to which we will respond with the usual stages of the grieving process: first of all denial, followed by anger, then bargaining, then depression, then acceptance. Our loss is complex—it is financial only in the most obvious and superficial of our experiences. Losing wealth wrecks lifestyles, damages health, causes anxiety, fear, confusion and stress. It may destroy families. We will go through cycles of personal grief as well as collective, societal grief. We will deny what is happening, pretending that recovery will come in three years. We will get angry with our politicians and leading financiers, who failed to prevent this reverse. We will bargain, trying to find some way to get back what we have lost, on whatever terms. We will probably also become depressed as we begin to realize that the kind of lives we have lost, we truly have lost. They will not come back.

Grieving is an inevitable process of life, an essential dimension of our human condition. It is not to be feared, but rather embraced with courage and compassion. It is also an opportunity for learning, a chance to question ourselves more deeply. However, it needs careful navigation—and now is a time for leaders who will help us to make that journey well. Of course, the temptation is to short-circuit the process, in an attempt to avoid the pain. This is my fear in these times. I am not convinced that we or our leaders have the courage to embrace our loss as deeply as we must. I'm afraid that they will seek (as they currently seem to be seeking) some way to prod the dying mule back into life. In fact, I'm afraid that they may actually manage to get the old beast back on its feet again, by some artificial means of resuscitation, but only to prolong its demise until a final, more painful collapse in the next few decades.

My hope, on the other hand, is that our leaders will recognize the times we live in. Death is the opportunity for a renewal of life. However, birth is never easy or painless: labour involves struggle and risk. We should bear in mind that bringing new life to birth can be difficult, protracted, even violent.

## The birth of the new?

What, then, are the seeds that may fund a new birth in our social ecology today? It is clear where one such vision may come from: the West finds itself dealing with a new power in fundamentalist Islam which it does not seem to be able to hold in check. There is no doubt that for many Muslims the idea of an *ummah* (the worldwide Muslim community) ruled by shari'ah law is an appealing one. However, we must understand that appeal in the broader context of our current social ecology, in which most Muslims see themselves as migrants and members of a global underclass. The presence of 'infidel' foreign troops in the holy land of Saudi Arabia throughout the 1990s and into the 2000s inflamed Muslim sensibilities. The backwardness of the economies of many Muslim countries in comparison with those of the West suggest a subservience that many Muslims find intolerable. The fundamentalist understanding of the global situation is of a territorial war between the forces of Christendom and those of 'the house of Islam' in which for three centuries the latter has been humiliated. The poor living standards of even moderate Muslims mean that, sadly, they are easily manipulated by the rhetoric of radical mullahs.

And here's the rub: those displaced, migrant populations are easily radicalized. Extremism flourishes wherever people are marginalized. It is no coincidence that a state such as Chechnya produces suicide bombers, women as well as men, who are willing to murder 340 schoolchildren. It is no coincidence that the recruitment of radical young Muslim men to radical versions of Islam is rising rapidly in our prison population. It is no coincidence that growing numbers of people at the poorer end of our society are converting to Islam. In certain Muslim communities around the world, there seems to be an endless supply of would-be suicide bombers. Their hearts and minds are so easily won over by rhetoric that promises revolution, power, authority, justice. Such desires are common to all those who occupy those positions in the social ecology—and when they are married with a religious ideology that glorifies martyrdom and promises an instant transfer to Paradise, it is not difficult to see how a death cult arises.

The Islamist vision is enjoying a strident and violent resurgence around the globe. It is a response to both the decline of the vision of Christendom and the ascendancy of the vision of a secular world. It is a response to a vision of humankind dominated by the market. Ultimately, however, as a territorial ideology, it is informed by a sense of fear rather than a sense of trust. And it is for this reason that it must be resisted, even as we look about for an alternative vision. Perhaps the greatest problem that faces the West is simply this: we no longer have a compelling ideological vision of our own.

Our liberal democracies and capitalist economies were products of the theological vision of the Renaissance. Such theological assumptions as that all people are created equal, as individuals with inherent creativity and the ability to work productively, provided the impulse for European civilization. And yet it has been the misapplication of those assumptions that has led us to the point of collapse: productivity without rest, aspiration without restraint, rights without responsibilities, freedoms without limits, ownership without stewardship. And the church has lost its voice as a critic of or contributor to our social health. It is seen either to be irrelevant to society or to be acquiescent to the status quo, giving its blessing to those already in power. For many, its theology has gone dry, its language cold; it is perceived to be just as territorial and political as radical Islam.

And yet human beings are spiritual beings. Whatever the materialist humanists may say, there is more to us than flesh and blood, brain and bone.

You are at liberty to disagree with me, and I will not try to prove that point. What I want to maintain is that there is an urgent need for the people in the West to rediscover this dimension of life. When we lack a spiritual perspective, we tend (with some notable exceptions) to become baser: less able to make sacrifices for others because our lives lack that sense of the eternal that makes sacrifice in this life possible. Our art, poetry, music and fiction tend to become more mundane, because the themes we have to explore are narrower and less deep. Our morality becomes more volatile and more opportunistic, because it is not anchored to any absolute values, and as a result it can easily be diverted in directions that are less costly to us. Our emotions become an end in themselves, and 'feeling good' becomes our ultimate goal, reducing the chances that we will persevere and grow through tragedy, loss and pain, or that we will aspire to act with courage in the noble cause.

Of course, these are generalizations: there are notable exceptions in every culture, men and women who have shown remarkable humanity even though they have rejected the idea of the human spirit in any theological sense. However, my observations are broadly true, and they make sense.

Contemporary spirituality, too, must not be completely separated from the tradition of practice and belief or else it becomes emptied of meaning. For example, it's increasingly fashionable in the West to combine elements of a variety of different spiritual traditions: a little Buddhism, a little Confucianism, a little shamanism, a little Christianity and so on. This pick'n'mix approach appeals to the liberal mind, but what it creates is something fragile and ultimately fairly worthless. The difficult bits of each spiritual tradition—and each of them has uncomfortable insights and disciplines—tend to be eliminated, and what remains is like a fruitcake composed entirely of cherries, a sickly self-indulgence. It has neither intellectual, emotional, moral nor historic rigour. It speaks of the worst kind of Western consumerism, for which spirituality is just another product to stick in your basket and enjoy at your leisure.

Human spirituality is not a sweet counter from which we can select whatever catches our eye. Such a creed of personal indulgence bears no relation to any of the ancient wisdoms that inform our major spiritual traditions. Nor can our spirituality be conceived simply as 'that which fulfils us'. Many spiritual traditions would contend that the fulfilment of our potential as human beings is a by-product of our spiritual journey, not the goal we struggle towards. We strive for something beyond ourselves—and, incidentally, in so doing we find ourselves becoming more human, more alive. However, to seek that as an end in itself (like searching for happiness as an end in itself) ultimately makes us less human, less alive, rather than more.

The Western spiritual tradition is derived predominantly from Christianity. It is clear that historically (whatever revisionist historians might want us to believe) the noblest ideals of our culture and its greatest achievements, both compassionate and creative, have been inspired by the life and teaching of Jesus of Nazareth. His followers have largely not lived up to his ideals, but Western society in all its aspects desperately needs to rediscover him and hear his voice again. This is true not least of the church, which in Europe continues to decline both in numbers and social and political influence. That said, the media have generally been hostile to the church in Europe and have been discrediting it for many decades—but that may soon change!

Is what we need, if we are to see a rebirth in our society, a renewed source of theology that is robust enough to fund an entire vision of life? A theology that can weave together the many different threads in the complex fabric of our society: the cultural and the aesthetic, the industrial and the economic, the social and the communitarian, the personal and the political, the emotional and the psychological, the traditional and the contemporary. To accomplish this will demand the commitment of people of faith in many different disciplines throughout our society.

## Study questions 9

1. What are the signs that the most recent cycle of social ecology is coming to an end?
2. Can technology save us? If not, why not?
3. Is the Western malaise due to a lack of ideology?
4. Why is spirituality fundamental to healthy human society?

# PART II

# RECONSTRUCTION:

# LESSONS FOR THE FUTURE OF SOCIETY

# TEN

## The Future Before It Unfolds

At its most basic, we in the West have to choose to live more interdependent lives. Our recent post-industrial history has seen the transformation of our society from one that promotes interdependence to one that promotes independence. Advances in technology, as well as the changes in outlook that have accompanied them, have encouraged us to look after ourselves. Almost every household is now self-contained, with its own water supply, its own means of transport, its own 'entertainment centre' and its own equipment for washing clothes, cooking, mowing the lawn and so on. We have all but completed a journey from the communal life of the medieval village to the extreme privacy of a modern home managed from a computer terminal, with minimal contact with people outside.

It is biology that has allowed this social isolation. Species that live in colonies or groups tend to be found in environments where resources are scarce: when there is little to go round, cooperation makes life easier. Living alone is a luxury usually affordable only to those who live in the midst of plenty and don't need others. In the last two hundred years, technology has given people in the West access to sufficient resources to mean that generally we do not need to cooperate with others in order to survive. Two centuries ago, entertainment might have involved singing folk songs together around a jar of ale; today, I can access all my hedonistic pleasures from the isolation of my computer screen. Transport generally involved sharing a vehicle; today I sit alone in my car, sealed off from other commuters around me. In the past, only the odd ascetic could survive living alone; nowadays, we are all adept at it.

### A blip in the history of the world?

However, people may one day look back on this period when we developed such isolated and independent patterns of living as a brief aberration. It is clear that the abundance of resources that made such a lifestyle possible is coming to an end. It is no coincidence, therefore, that the new movements that are developing in the West by and large have a collectivist vision. Groups promoting sustainable lives and renewable energies almost invariably encourage collaboration. For example, for economies of scale to make solar or wind power affordable, local housing communities may need to commit to building something communal. Some new housing developments share waste energy to heat everyone's houses and recycle everyone's used water to flush the toilets. As the resources available to us dwindle, so we will find ourselves looking for more cooperative ways to maintain our standard of living together. Our natural human response to the environmental crisis will be to become more social and cohesive again. 'Interdependence' will be the new buzzword, not 'independence'.

A growing number of 'eco projects' are beginning to emerge, in everything from housing (including community living) to schooling to manufacturing to energy production to the arts, and to be seen as an acceptable alternative to the mainstream. Indeed, increasing numbers of ordinary people will find that these developments appeal to something inside them, a growing desire for a life that is more authentic, more holistic, more honest, more simple, more connected. Here is the germ of a new, compelling, radical collectivist vision which, once it is sown in our hearts, will begin to take root there.

## Warnings and lessons for 'developing' economies

While Western societies are concerned with halting the disintegration of their civic structure and the loss of their social capital, those of the majority world are in the grip of increasing individualism. It is almost as if as the West comes down from the peak of its individualism, the East is climbing towards its own peak—and at some point they will reach parity. Certainly there will be terrible costs if the majority world follows the same path as the West. These would be incurred primarily by the peoples of the majority world, in terms of their social cohesion and well-being. This book is a health warning to all those who imagine that all is well in the West and want to emulate it.

The appeal the Western model has for people in 'developing' economies is not hard to understand. All kinds of desire come into play:

- to attain economic parity with the minority world
- to enjoy the status and prestige associated with being a First World economy
- to make the most of your country's talent and capital
- to improve yourself and your country
- to reduce poverty
- to possess the advantages and opportunities available to people in the West
- to offer your people a better life

However, these very proper aspirations all entail costs. Let me spell out, by way of a summary of the argument from the previous eight chapters, what these might be.

- increasing political domination by a corporatocracy
- a breakdown of the extended-but-local family
- an increase in dependence on the state and a growing unemployable underclass
- a decline in trust and informal community, and no increase in popular participation in democratic politics
- a decline in mental health and an associated rise in costs
- no discernable increase in the 'gross national happiness'
- an increasing burden on the state to care for a growing proportion of the unemployable or elderly
- a fragile economy dependent on a small sector of the population and vulnerable to shifts in macro-economic patterns
- a loss of professional talent to service-sector employment (call centres etc)
- increasing materialism, and an associated decrease in spiritual awareness
- increasing social instability, resulting in a growing sense of insecurity among the better off and of injustice among the rest
- a long-term crisis as more and more basic foodstuffs and other resources are imported rather than being produced locally
- the selling-off of the country's assets to foreign businesses
- growing inflationary pressure, reducing the buying power of the (growing) average wealth
- growing pressure to manage the size of the population
- a loss of indigenous culture, replaced by a homogeneous global McCulture shaped by corporate brands

The benefits are clear, but so is the evidence from Western experience that they do not come without their attendant costs. Is there, maybe, a way of enabling economic development that avoids those costs? If there is, perhaps it offers a vision and a direction not just for the 'developing' economies but also for those that are 'already developed'. Perhaps there are lessons to be learned by the leaders of the West as well as those of the East.

## *Key questions for global society*

The second part of this book is a response to the analysis in Part I. The danger in attempting to offer specific suggestions for action is that, on the one hand, if they are too specific they begin to sound like a political manifesto, but, on the other hand, if they are too general they are open to the criticism that they are too imprecise. I want to try to avoid both traps. This is not a political manifesto, in that I believe that each society will have to work out the relevance to its own particular situation of the principles I set out.

Part II, then, returns to the structure of the social ecology that has shaped my analysis in Part I. Using the same methodology, I will ask how each of the eight sectors of a social ecology can be deliberately managed to ensure the good of the whole. The goal is to describe a way in which a social system can grow for the benefit of all, stable and sustainable, offering opportunity to all with justice, compassion and generosity. There are eight key questions we must ask ourselves:

1. RSC: What are the key elements that ensure strong moral and cultural foundations?
2. PWX: How can you direct consumers' aspirations so that they invest in social as well as financial capital growth?
3. PSC: How can you create a thriving private-sector economy that participates responsibly in the wider society?
4. RWX: How can you enable migration while preventing instability and exploitation?
5. PSX: How can you make sure that people who excel in disciplines that are important for society are properly celebrated, in order to encourage aspiration in those disciplines?
6. RWC: What key policies ensure that the underclass receives compassionate support without becoming dependent on the state?
7. PWC: How do you foster social cohesion in an aspirational society?
8. RSX: What is the role of faith in social well-being, and what are its dangers?

It is the responsibility of the leaders of societies around the world to address all eight of these questions and find an answer to them. If they fail to do so, they are culpable for whatever harm ensues. Everyone has the right to expect that their society's leaders—economic and political, in education and in the community—have reflected hard on each of these questions, because they relate to the basic components of every society's health.

## *Global questions, local applications*

Although these questions are applicable worldwide, their application can only be worked out locally. I have written this book largely from a Western perspective—my home is in Western Europe. Many of the applications I suggest in the chapters that follow are relevant only to that particular context and are not intended as universal to all other societies. It is simply impossible for any one book to provide applications across many different cultures and societies.

My hope is that what follows will stimulate you to work out your own local answers. The website hosts a forum, on which are posted substantial responses from leaders in different parts of the globe. If we treat this forum as a smithy, where we can all bring our best ideas to be heated up in the fire and then hammered into shape, I hope it will produce many worthwhile and effective instruments of social change.

## *Study questions 10*

1. Why has Western society been able to foster such independence, in contrast to all other human societies throughout history?
2. Is such independence sustainable?
3. What are the costs associated with it, to society and its members?

# ELEVEN

## Culture and Nationalism

## (RSC, Foundational)

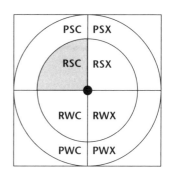

**Key question: What are the key elements that ensure strong moral and cultural foundations?**

**Key principle:**

*Rebuilding a strong and resilient social ecology begins with reconstructing its foundations. This is a matter of identifying the values and beliefs, the stories and traditions, that underpin the society and strengthening them. This is not something that can be done by government—though legislation can create favourable conditions for such an endeavour.*

There are two elements that are essential to the establishing of strong moral and cultural foundations. One is a sense of attachment to a particular time and a particular place. The other is a sense of belonging to something that is bigger and older than we are in being part of a community that shares the same pattern of life. These two ingredients need to be present throughout the mix of society. We feel a sense of belonging when we observe the same rhythms as everyone around us—and those rhythms also draw attention to the things our society values. If everyone is allowed to do whatever they like with their own time, it implies that there is no such thing as society.

## *Suggestions for application*

### Strengthening the family

Children learn how to behave morally by watching how adults behave, chiefly in their own families. The family is the crucial milieu where social and moral norms are passed on. If it breaks down, these norms have to be transmitted through the education system, which is more (and more) expensive, involves the state and is not such an appropriate environment as the family. When children enjoy consistent relationships in their early years with caregivers in the family, it give them a sense of identity and enables them to grow up into emotionally stable adults. Maintaining and strengthening those relationships is arguably the most important task any government has to perform.

A society could assess its own general well-being by examining how stable its family structures were. The key indicators of the strength of its foundations are the resilience of family bonds, the status of marriage and how long relationships between parents last.

Financial incentives, including tax breaks, are essential to support the family and promote lifelong monogamous relationships.

## Encouraging common stories

People also need to feel that they belong within a tradition and a history. 'Who am I?' is a question that cannot be answered fully unless you know where you have come from and what your family, your community and your nation all say about themselves. Having such stories passed down to them gives people a sense of security in the uncertainty of the present. However, every society needs to encourage us to tell these stories constructively and responsibly. Stories about the family or the group can become exclusive and divisive, promoting a kind of tribalism, unless they are contained within a bigger, national story, a story in which everyone has a commitment to common values and practices, submits to common laws and accepts the limitation of their own personal freedom for the common good.

Multiculturalism has to be tempered by a recognition that every nation needs a dominant cultural story that its members can find a role within. That doesn't mean there will be no room for individuals to be different in their beliefs and tastes and dress and so on, but nonetheless the nation should be like a huge family and there should be a recognizable family likeness between all its members and each individual should have a sense of belonging and commitment to it. Like any family, it offers privileges—affection, security, opportunity—as well as responsibilities.

This implies a degree of loyalty to the national 'family', a willingness to see other members of the nation in terms of 'us' rather than 'them' and an acceptance of the disciplines that membership of that family entails (which includes recognizing its authorities and limiting our dissent to 'the proper channels'). Our membership of that national family is rarely under threat—but it can be.

At the same time, the national family celebrates the differences between its members and encourages them to learn from each other, to regard each other as friends and to work together on common tasks.

## Encouraging local commitment

Arguably, it is essential also to discourage excessive mobility and encourage people to make a long-term commitment to their local communities. This would have an impact on town and city planning, with regard (for example) to the location of shopping, leisure and essential facilities to enable people to work, shop and socialize close to where they live. It should also affect public housing policy, as tenants who have no stake in their state-owned homes have less commitment to them and their neighbourhoods. Schemes that enable people to own or part-own their homes encourage them to put down roots and get involved in the local community.

## Investing festivals with meaning

Festivals and national holidays give us an opportunity to 'remind ourselves who we are'.

If a particular religion plays a part in a society's story, there should be an explicit (though maybe not exclusive) role for its festivals in that society's life. They should be offered sensitively to every member of that society, whether or not she follows that faith herself; but they should not be 'fudged', or their meaning or origin obscured, simply to avoid giving offence to non-believers. Once again, if a society is dominated by one particular religion, it should expect everyone to celebrate its festivals, whether that be Christmas, Diwali or Ramadan.

If we allow businesses to determine how a whole society celebrates its festivals, we imply that buying and selling are our top priorities. If we allow the state to dictate how individuals should use their time, we imply that ordinary people can't be trusted. What we want to promote is the idea that people should participate in the dominant culture because it is part of the foundations of their society. The rhythms of public life in any society should be determined not by commercial interests or government say-so but by the bigger common cultural stories that inform that society.

# TWELVE

## Consumption and Citizenship

### (PWX, Aspirational)

**Key question: How can you direct consumers' aspirations so that they invest in social as well as financial capital growth?**

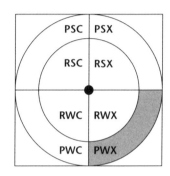

**Key principle:**

*Human beings are by nature aspirational. Our desire for more or better will not abate, but rather needs to be channelled so that we seek to acquire more of the right kind of things. This involves an understanding of the psychology of desire and fulfilment, so that as a society we can encourage people to aspire to that which is, in social terms, sustainable and healthy.*

There is no doubt that ultimately the challenge that faces humankind is to reduce our total consumption—and that this must begin with the West. All but the wealthiest Westerners will, almost certainly, have to reduce their consumption of energy and other resources over the next 40 years, if not voluntarily, because we are compelled to by rising prices. However, no elected government is likely to introduce substantial 'green' taxes or a system in which we trade carbon credits like money, or legislate for fair trade internationally or enforce other major changes in our lifestyles. Certainly it is inconceivable that any democracy will embrace the idea of a shrinking economy. All of these may be necessary to secure the future of our civilization, if not our species—and yet it would be electoral suicide for any government to propose them.

In order to build up our social (as opposed to financial) capital and to develop the will to discipline our own lifestyles, we need to take account of the way human beings make decisions at an emotional level. We make choices that make us feel better. We act to reduce our feelings of guilt and sadness, confusion and fear and to increase our happiness and our sense that we have meaning and are loved and are secure. For the past century, our societies have believed that we can achieve all this through amassing financial capital while cheerfully sacrificing our social capital. We need to turn this around so that we expect to attain those same goals by amassing social capital even if it means losing financial capital.

Given that over the coming decades we have to manage a reduction in our consumption of the world's resources, the role of politics will be to enable civic society to adjust to the new constraints while maintaining order, confidence and a sense of shared identity. The change needs to be negotiated rather than revolutionary. At present, this message is as unwelcome as the news that you have won a million dollars would be thrilling. The trick—and it is a trick—is to work out how to help people to adjust to what at first sight looks like a painful future they will want to avert.

Our ideas about happiness are largely mistaken, as recent research has found. We often believe that things will make us happy which actually will not. Some research suggests that the part of our brain that registers desire (for money, sex, power or whatever) is disconnected from the part that registers pleasure. This may explain why we continue to pursue things in the belief that they will fulfil our desires, only to be disappointed. Of course, this fallacy is the whole basis of consumerism! The aim of every advertisement and every product placement is to excite desire in us, to make us want something we don't yet have: it trades on the apparent disconnection between those two parts of the brain. If they were hardwired up to each other, we would feel genuinely satisfied once we had bought the thing we desired, full stop—and that would spell the end of fashion, of 'product lifecycles', of brand marketing, of advertising. The entire capitalist edifice is, in a sense, built on the lack of communication between two different parts of our brains, and a misreading of ourselves and our world.

Given that we are never going to be able to rewire our brains, however, we have to learn to live with this problem and deal with it as best we can. Studies such as the one cited above should help to guide us as we consider how to prepare Western society for less financial wealth and lower consumption.

## *Managing expectations*

Reductions in overall salary levels may not hurt us as much as we fear at first, but our sense that we are getting less than our peers will demoralize us. In other words, our sense of disappointed hope and even injustice will create negative emotion.

If, however, we were hearing from our politicians now that incomes are likely to fall and we need to start saving now, I believe we would adjust to this new prospect fairly rapidly and well. We would tighten our belts and get on with it, I suspect—and when the hit came we would be ready for it, and might even be pleasantly surprised if we ended up a little better off that we had expected. It is our expectations, in other words, that need to be managed.

There is no evidence to suggest that a population living on less will be any unhappier than we are now, or that the political party that presided over that change would be punished at the polls. What matters is how expectations about that change is handled. What we need now is greater honesty about what lies in store for us, rather than desperate prevarication in the hope that some other politician or government will have to break the bad news.

## Changing the consensus on consumption

There may be a case for extending the regulation of the advertising and marketing we are all exposed to. Most of us are comfortable with this in relation to products that are now considered to be toxic or otherwise a danger to health. The health warnings on cigarette packets are placed there to dampen our desires; product and warning happily coexist within a free market. Warnings against unprotected sex and drink-driving serve the same function.

Likewise, government warnings about the cost in carbon emissions of unnecessary journeys by car or plane, for example, or of food that has travelled thousands of miles to reach the shop where we buy it, might not change our behaviour necessarily but would help to alter public perceptions of what is and is not socially acceptable. They would bring into play such feelings as shame and respect, which Western governments have rarely appealed to in recent decades.

## Redeploying taxation

The most effective and realistic way to control the market generates revenue to pay for public services while at the same time imposing a heavy financial cost on the consumer. It's appropriate in a free society that, within reasonable limits, we can choose how to use our own resources, and yet none of our choices are consequence-free. How we use water, energy, food, fuel and so on has an effect on everyone else. Those resources are limited, and the limits are now being reached. Taxing personal spending rather than personal wealth generation may be a more precise way to control consumption while maintaining people's motivation to work and be productive. Taxation should also reflect the fact that we are taking resources from a finite system—for example, by taxing us on the 'carbon footprint' we leave on our global ecological system.

## *Rewarding those who build up social capital*

At the same time as managing the reduction in our consumption, we need policies that will foster and reward the building-up of social capital. If those positive feelings of affection, fulfilment and happiness are no longer focused on the act of consuming, there needs to be some reward mechanism to give people an incentive to promote social cohesion. For example, it is still shocking that in Britain if you are a married parent and you are staying at home to bring up your children, current taxation policy will make you worse off than you would be if you were an unmarried parent doing the same—and worse off than you would be, married or not, if you hired a childminder and went out to work.[59] The taxation system needs to favour those who make a commitment to their family and their local community—and hence to social cohesion—rather than penalizing them.

## *Recognizing and rewarding voluntary care*

I remember a newspaper interview of a feminist author in 2006 who said that one unexpected consequence of feminism had been its negative impact on elderly people. As a boy, I used to accompany my mother while she took 'meals on wheels' to people who were infirm and housebound. We used to visit old folk in the village every week as a matter of course, just to check that they were OK (and stay for a chat). Sunday lunch in those days was more often than not shared with someone in need from the village. For all my parents' compassion, this kind of local care (replicated by others all over the country) was possible only because my mother had no paid employment. Instead of generating financial capital for her family, she generated social capital for the local community. For this, the state was in her debt. She greatly reduced the burden on the health and welfare services, as well as teaching me the responsibility of those of working age for the elderly.

Sadly, examples like that of my mother are rarely seen these days and are hardly valued. Of course, she paid a price: in later life she was unable to get back into the career she was pursuing before she got married, and she also found herself excluded by the 'professionalization' of all the skills she had to offer. She lived through the transition from a society that believed in and encouraged informal social care for the needy and the old to one whose subservience to a rapacious growing economy has meant that more and more vulnerable people

---

[59] Stuart Adam and James Browne, *A Survey of the UK Tax System*, Institute for Fiscal Studies briefing note 9, 2006 (http://www.ifs.org.uk/bns/bn09.pdf); John Elliott and Claire Newell, 'Why Can't They Be Left Alone?', *The Sunday Times*, 17 June 2007 (http://www.timesonline. co.uk/tol/news/politics/article1942935.ece)

struggle alone, their relations spread out all over the country, while most of the female population is at work. Though overall standards of living have risen as a result of this change, 'gross national happiness' has not—and, given the colossal inflation we have seen in the housing market especially, most of the money has simply gone to the Exchequer.

Without the foresight to see the impact on our social ecology of such economic policies and the ideologies behind them, we have suffered the inevitable consequences of losing the attitudes that led people to practise compassion and promoted social cohesion. Now we have to pay for the care they used to give out of the (inflated) public purse. Help from the state has tended merely to replace private charity rather than supplementing it, and is certainly not an improvement on it. Once again, we could hope to produce some social change through the mechanism of the market, by creating a tax system that rewarded stable families, rewarded those who stay at home to bring up their children and rewarded those who are voluntary carers.

# THIRTEEN

## Capital

## (PSC, Dominant Norm)

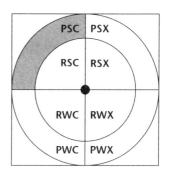

**Key question: How can you create a thriving private-sector economy that participates responsibly in social commitment?**

**Key principle:**

*We urgently need to restructure the relationship between private and collective ownership. We have seen them almost exclusively as antithetical alternatives, and this polarization has allowed the private sector to become detached from suppliers, stakeholder communities and even the environment. There are other forms of ownership that need to be properly explored. Corporate social responsibility needs to become a universal and central element of business models and practice rather than being just a sideshow.*

Since the Second World War, the politics of the West has been dominated by the drive for economic growth. Given the state of the European economies in 1945, such a priority then was understandable. However, this has come at a cost to our larger social and spiritual welfare. Broadly speaking, the growth in our GDPs has been facilitated by the spread of an individualism that has allowed an unfettered expansion of the free market, encouraged enterprise and boosted spending. This has had a number of unforeseen consequences:

- a narrow view of what we value (assessed almost exclusively in financial terms)
- a narrow understanding of corporate ownership, exclusively in financial terms
- the detaching of the supplier from the customer, so that the transaction between them is merely functional and contractual

- the unlinking of corporate salary levels from any meaningful sense of appropriate scale
- a reluctance in governments to impose regulations for fear of being seen as hostile to free-market economics
- an excessive confidence in the market's ability both to regulate itself and to address social ills
- a false polarization between capitalist and collectivist ideas of ownership
- an unfortunate and inappropriate transference of private-sector methods and measures to the public, not-for-profit and professional sectors

## *Exploring alternative models of corporate ownership*

It would be a mistake to think that we can solve the problem of the dominance of capital through either centralized control or radical socialism: neither autocracy nor communism has shown that it can foster more just social structures. However, what needs to be addressed here is the question of who actually owns a company. Clearly, its shareholders are among its owners—but so, surely, do the local communities in whose neighbourhoods the company operates, so do the suppliers who provide it with materials, so do the employees who make its products or deliver its services, so do the consumers who buy them and represent the company's brand to the world. The notion of ownership is complex—far more multifaceted than our current shareholder system suggests. We have to challenge current assumptions about it and get the debate going.

This will immediately strike a chill of fear into the heart of every corporate executive and share owner in the land: fear of losing their financial worth, fear of losing control. It will be argued that to redefine company ownership would inevitably make a company harder to direct, less efficient, less productive, less able to compete in the global market. However, there are examples of different models of ownership that have not only survived but actually thrived in the commercial world. Think of the British retailer John Lewis/Waitrose. Its founding principle is that every one of its employees is a partner in the firm. Every one, from the chair to the most junior cashier, receives the same percentage of their salary as their end-of-year bonus. As a plaque on the wall of the firm's central offices reminds them each day: 'In 1914 John Spedan Lewis laid the foundations for a different kind of business. His vision was of a great commercial enterprise whose success would be measured by the happiness of those working in it and by its good service to the general community.' In 2006, John Lewis/Waitrose had 64,000 partners and turned over six billion euros.

Think, too, of the radical example of ownership of intellectual capital presented by the software company Linux. Its software is written by volunteers and is not sold but 'given away'—an example of 'freeware', observing the 'copyleft' principle of intellectual ownership. The firm generates profits through service contracts and relies on the personal enthusiasm of its contributors, whose reward comes from being part of a creative enterprise. Wikipedia operates on similar principles, and both enterprises are challenging assumptions that products such as theirs will suffer from poor quality if their authors are not contracted, managed and paid along more familiar commercial lines.

John Lewis/Waitrose and Linux present models of ownership that intentionally capitalize on trust and partnership; they build up social capital as well as amassing financial capital. Nor are they alone. There is the Co-operative group of businesses, which includes a chain of supermarkets, a bank, a travel agency and a funeral business. More controversial is eBay, which exploits the way the internet facilitates feedback to create a community of trust without the usual contracts. Meanwhile, the microfinance industry is an astonishing way in which financial capital can be wedded with the building and developing of social capital in the developing world. Perhaps the emergence of social entrepreneurship heralds the dawn of a new era of capitalist endeavour.

- There are undoubtedly models available in which social and financial capital are enabled to grow together rather than competing against each other.
- Business schools must do more thinking on models of capital ownership so that such approaches can become mainstream management practice rather than something alternative on the fringe.
- What we need is a sea change in thinking that will leave behind the instinctive individualism that has marked the West since the Enlightenment.

Collectivism cannot be simply another reaction to individualism: it needs to become the prevailing paradigm within which we understand currency, value and growth.

## *Reconnecting business with the local poor*

Many successful Western firms are now recognizing that their commitment to integrity (whether ethical or financial) is strengthened as they deepen their relationship with their local community and its concerns. This fosters affection, compassion and a sense of common humanity that crosses boundaries. How much easier it is for a business to make a commitment to reducing its energy consumption, or to paying its suppliers a fairer price or to setting up a mentoring scheme for local teenagers, if its employees vote to do so as a result of their own encounters with poverty and deprivation in the local (or global) community! If we can find ways for companies to reconnect with the wider social ecology, it will initiate a virtuous circle that will in time help to make possible a variety of policy shifts and structural changes that currently are unthinkable.

- Increasingly in the West, younger people in the workforce are motivated not by money alone but by a desire for authenticity: they want to believe that what they do makes some contribution to society, that it has meaning and value beyond the stock market. Increasingly, businesses recognize that 'employee engagement' means that the firm itself needs to engage in meaningful activity.

- For some companies, corporate social responsibility, or CSR, seems to be little more than a PR exercise at present—there is little evidence that, if it came to the crunch, it would be allowed actually to affect their strategic objectives or their share value. However, the very fact that they feel the need to pursue CSR for PR purposes shows they are aware that the wider society sees the commercial world as exploitative.

## The best way to 'develop' employees: CSR

Some CSR projects involve businesses releasing employees periodically to help in local social projects. Think of the skills there are in the City of London, in Canary Wharf, in other commercial centres around the world! A small fraction of those skills lent to local communities would have a significant effect in terms of creating trust, imparting knowledge and empowerment. Think of the mentoring that could be offered young black and Asian entrepreneurs! Think of the talent that might be saved from going down the drain if those young men and women were given direction and training and role models worth imitating—and not by some government scheme but by a commitment to the community made by the private sector! Think how much more enriching it would be for middle managers to be involved in a leadership development programme alongside local community, religious or business leaders, rather than doing yet another team-building exercise in some dull hotel suite! The evidence is that the rising generation is a generation of pragmatists and activists: people who want to get on and do something. Their talents are best developed by engaging them in some cause.

- There is a tremendous opportunity, as traditional voluntary organizations find it harder to recruit, for businesses to benefit from releasing their own employees to community service. The 'benefit flow' will be far from one-way. Indeed, it may well be that it is the companies' staff who are most enriched by such encounters. The broadening of their horizons may give them 'out-of-the-box' experiences worth 10 traditional management-training events. Moreover, this is not aid, or patronage, or the company 'giving away' the percentage of its profit it can afford to lose in a tax-efficient PR stunt (though it will no doubt include all of those things as well). Fundamentally, it is an investment, not in financial capital but in social capital. What is being built up is trust, that precious commodity that binds human beings together; that almost always reduces the cost of human transactions, changing contracts into covenants; that simply begins with people talking and listening to each other, discovering common ground, finding that they can be friends and not strangers.

Ultimately, if the City were to commit itself to this kind of enterprise, both in London and around the world, within a decade the benefits would be enormous. Private capital would be 'tied' once again to social responsibility. The opposite poles of our social ecology, PSC and RWX, which are currently in opposition to each other, would be brought closer together. Goodwill would be generated, common concerns would emerge and all kinds of small projects that would benefit both the local community and the company would spring up. The loss of 'office time' would be amply repaid by the energy, motivation, creativity and humanity that such initiatives would generate in the office. Businesses would find themselves better able to solve their own internal problems of lack of trust because they had gained experience of trusting other people with very different backgrounds and perspectives.

## *Defending corporate assets from private collectors*

Publicly listed companies are subject to financial audit and regulation. Recently, however, the development of private equity funds has allowed such companies to escape public scrutiny by enabling them to be bought by small consortia of investors who are not subject to the same rules. These funds are inimical to the broader health of the economy because they remove wealth even further from public accountability. Many commentators suggest that these funds make a very small number of people very rich while stripping companies of their assets. It is fairly clear that the owners of private equity funds don't want to buy up public companies in order to make them more open, responsible and socially committed.

# FOURTEEN

## Control and Capacity

# (RWX, Migrant)

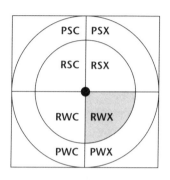

**Key question: How can you enable migration while preventing instability and exploitation?**

**Key principle:**

*Large numbers of immigrants can be absorbed successfully only by a society that has a robust and resilient culture. Without this, the host society will be damaged and the very things that attracted the migrants in the first place will be destroyed.*

There is a crucial difference between a multiracial society and a multicultural society. In the former, people of several different races coexist within a single culture; in the latter, two or more different cultures coexist within one society. In the West, we have come to accept the ideal of a multicultural society, but I suggest that we should, in fact, embrace the ideal of a multiracial one. I believe there are negative consequences to trying to create a multicultural society, which has no single host culture but only a number of equally valid cultures, all competing.

In Britain, we have made the mistake of supposing that giving people freedom from rules and boundaries is a generous act that will liberate them. Instead, it has left them bewildered and insecure. Many people from ethnic minorities fail to find their way out of the RWX migrant niche—which breeds resentment and prejudice and arguably has helped to light the fire of radical Islam. The power structure is completely unstable.

## Make the host culture a cohesive force

What is urgently needed now is for Britain's host culture to recover its self-confidence, so that it can redraw its boundaries and rebuild its walls, setting out its values and beliefs so that immigrants can orientate themselves. It must have a distinctive form in which everyone participates positively.

Part of this involves making clear the conditions (RSC) for belonging to the host culture. Such conditions create expectations, create security for the vulnerable and the innocent; they keep out those people who would vandalize or otherwise spoil the environment, and welcome in those who want to make a positive contribution. They provide a stable power structure, as all reserved, strong, consolidating (RSC) elements do. Imposing conditions of entry for asylum seekers and other immigrants and deciding the number of immigrants the country will accept are measures concerned not with exclusion so much as with the protection of those who genuinely want to participate in the society, and a healthy balance of power.

## Don't exploit immigrants for short-term gain

Western Europe is suffering a demographic crisis: birth rates are falling and so populations are ageing, obliging people to work harder to maintain economic growth and to retire later. In some countries, the 'deficit' is being met by immigration and imported labour. However, such policies are dangerously short-term, storing up problems of social integration, pressure on the infrastructure and burdens on state services, benefits systems, the education system and so on. Merely the cost of providing translation services to local authorities for hundreds of thousands of immigrant families is unsustainable. Immigration itself is not a problem—but integration is. Our leaders must consider what conditions we impose on immigrants to foster a social system that is stable in the long term without embedding injustice and abuse.

## Diversity can flourish only on a foundation of conformity

Only when a society has a strong cultural foundation can it entertain and accommodate alien cultures, which find themselves secure and respected because they enjoy a relationship with the dominant, foundational (RSC) culture, not because they have supplanted it. Without that relationship, they become insecure, volatile and vulnerable. The ideology known as political correctness, which favours the minority as an end in itself and maintains that any majority is self-evidently oppressive and discriminatory, is specious and dangerous. It undermines the very resilience of the host culture that originally attracted the immigrants. In truth, minorities are made secure when they appreciate the foundational host culture in which they have found a safe space (RSC). They are not allowed to develop in isolation, without reference to that culture, or in contradiction of its values. They answer their host's generosity with their own generosity, sharing their own good life just as they have received the good life that exists within the host culture. They recognize that the freedom they have to live and act on the front stage (PWX) of society is guaranteed to them, as to us, only by the foundations that exist 'backstage' (RSC).

# FIFTEEN

## Celebrity

## (PSX, Iconic)

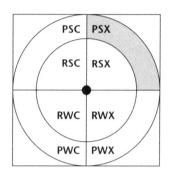

**Key Question: How can you make sure that people who excel in disciplines that are important for society are properly celebrated, in order to encourage aspiration in those disciplines?**

**Key Principle:**

*Celebrity fulfils an important aspirational function within society. That being so, it cannot be left to the market to define the character of cultural icons. Society must exert some control over the kinds of people who are given the status of icons.*

We in the West have been consumed by the aspiration to own more, and by that we mean to own more money and then buy more goods with it. This aspirational drive relates to how we experience happiness. The recent research I have cited indicates that, inasmuch as people find happiness in how much they possess, it is not because they are rich per se but because they are richer than others around them. Being human, we compare ourselves with others in our group—and we see wealth and property merely as signs that indicate social ranking. An inflation of consumption occurs when some members of a small group see others 'getting ahead' and, temporarily, feeling better about themselves as a result while everyone else feels slightly worse. Those who have been 'left behind' then acquire the lifestyle accessories that indicate that they have caught up in the social rankings. Thus, the sum of the group's possessions increases but the sum of its members' happiness does not. Happiness is related not to our possessions themselves but to the messages they convey to us about our social standing within a community, a company or a society.

Happiness is a fairly basic human emotion, and one we cannot fundamentally change. We need instead to employ it to create not consumptive but social inflation—in other words, an inflation of social capital that in turn generates a rise in social standing. To a degree, we see this among the super-rich, when (for example) they become involved in 'philanthropic game-playing', competing to see who can give away the most millions. At this level of wealth the giving is largely cost-free, but it offers the giver a certain status within the social economy of the elite. Much more could be done by both the state and the media to encourage such aspirational generosity.

## *An essential tool for fostering social aspiration*

It is for this reason that I believe passionately in the value of a national broadcaster. One of the most widely celebrated services available to the global community is the BBC World Service. Alongside this, the British Broadcasting Corporation provides four television channels for its domestic audience, and a large number of radio stations. As a national broadcaster, it has both an obligation and the resources to broadcast material that promotes the good of society rather than the good of shareholders. It has the potential to inform the nation's consciousness and to be a powerful agent for the development of social capital. All this is beyond commercial broadcasters, who will always produce material designed to sensationalize, entertain and sell.

It is no coincidence that the BBC is still regarded around the world as a model of good broadcasting or that it has a highly effective consultancy arm that assists other countries (and, in particular, majority-world countries in the process of establishing a democracy) in developing their own national broadcasting services. These states understand the value of a public service broadcaster in supporting a healthy social system. It is my contention that if we bind the RSX (visionary and artistic) and PSX (iconic and celebrity) elements of our society to its RSC foundations, we can build a robust, self-reforming society that is open to change and innovation and yet has strong roots. When this connection is broken and instead the PSX element of a society is linked to the market, it acts like a disease, infecting and weakening society.

Imagine if television shows spotlit the lives of people who were living both elegantly and efficiently, committed to their local communities and causes. How much more enriching than the endless drivel of talk shows featuring social delinquents, D-list celebrity reality-TV shows and makeover shows! Imagine if we began to create a culture of celebrity icons whose fame rested not on their talent alone but on their good citizenship: if we promoted sporting heroes who committed a significant proportion of their time and money to the community, and artists who were funded by public money to produce art that dealt with the real issues of our day rather than the often vacuous and largely obscure stuff that fills most of our contemporary galleries. The state has a role in fostering responsible icons—the days when we could allow the market to determine the character and type of our social icons are surely over. It may be an axiom of the free market and the media that the market generates its own heroes, but why should we let the market dictate the rules of our society? We all pay a price when our celebrities live empty, mean-spirited, financially-inflated lives—our own souls are suffocated and our aspirations are reduced to mere greed.

## Society, not the market, must fashion our heroes

We must encourage the emergence of a new kind of hero: a PSX who is valued for what they achieve and what they give, not for the size of their augmented breasts or the way they kick a football. We have allowed the market to dictate whom we idolize. The market is responsible for the grotesque salaries paid to Premiership footballers (obeying the simple economic law of supply and demand). The market is responsible for the idealization of celebrities. The market is responsible for the craving we have for a lifestyle like that of the rich and famous, and for our own five minutes in the spotlight on some reality show. The market defines our heroes, and in the process renders them worthless.

Society, rather than the market, must fashion our heroes. It is in sports such as football, in which there is little incentive to perform for one's country, that the greatest inequities lie. In contrast, the Olympic Games link the performance of the individual to their nation—and those sports in which the funding athletes receive is related to their performance in the great international competitions, rather than in private and commercial club competitions, often produce the more dignified, modest and impressive competitors. When sport relies largely on state rather than private funding, it can demand a certain level of discipline, performance and behaviour from its practitioners and, in so doing, can produce worthy heroes who are dedicated, unassuming and possessed of a proper sense of self-worth and gratitude, and who exhibit values that a nation's youth need to aspire to. In contrast, for example, the pampered footballers of the Premiership lack virtually any values to which I would want my children to aspire.

## Arts funding should favour the life-enhancing

Much the same can be said of the arts as of sport. Britain's experience has shown that when the state under-invests in artists, we remove any incentive for our artists to produce work that is of social value, so that it is often what is radical, sensationalist and, frequently, destructive that is applauded. A society needs storytellers, writers and artists who will produce work for which society will be thankful.

# SIXTEEN

## Compassion

## (RWC, Underclass)

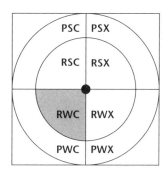

**Key Question: What key policies ensure that the underclass receives compassionate support without becoming dependent on the state?**

**Key Principle:**

*The contribution of the third sector, and in particular of faith-based voluntary organizations, needs to be recognized in the provision of welfare. Resources should be directed through such channels, while the public should appreciate that welfare is finite and not unconditional.*

One might measure the health of a society by its generosity and the protection it affords the vulnerable. However, compassion can easily encourage dependency. Support for those in need needs to be allied to programmes of rehabilitation. State-funded schemes also run into problems unless they find local partners. Nonetheless, a broader culture of compassion for the vulnerable must be fostered.

## *The crucial contribution of faith-based communities*

The most important contributors to social care are local voluntary bodies, and the most important of these are drawn from faith communities. Some people will find this statement provocative. Yet, problems the state is unable to solve are best addressed by just such communities. Many social issues in deprived areas can be dealt with only by agencies that are there for the long haul. The problem with government-funded social initiatives is that their funding is always vulnerable to changes in the political agenda. Usually money is made available for specific purposes and has particular conditions attached to its use, regardless of whether or not those conditions are relevant locally. Moreover, it may be withdrawn if social policy changes—as it so often does—because politicians need to demonstrate commitment to another 'hot' target.

Faith-based community schemes—whether to help the homeless or care for the elderly, provide youth services, run soccer teams or mentoring programmes or give advice about debt—can work much better, for two reasons. First, they are not generated from money from central or local government, and the people who fund them do so out of a long-term commitment to the area. That means such initiatives are best placed to make an effective contribution to social cohesion. Second, such communities can direct their resources at particular local needs rather than those dictated by some national target-based government initiative.

## Invest in faith-based schemes that serve unconditionally

In the past, people have voiced the suspicion that faith-based local services are merely a cover for evangelization, and as a result funds have been withheld that would most justly and efficiently have been allocated to their work. Such decisions have been unnecessary and short-sighted, influenced by the dogma of political correctness, which maintains that service providers should have no vested interest, no convictions, if they are to warrant funding. This fails to recognize that every organization has a vested interest and a conviction that drive their mission, not least the Government's own politically motivated work. The question is not what beliefs a particular group has but whether or not it is able and willing to serve the whole community without discrimination on ethnic or ideological lines.

The Government desperately needs to foster and support faith-based schemes that will serve the whole community unconditionally. Often, such projects are run on a shoestring by volunteers, while the state-funded youth work down the road (for example) is lavishly funded but often misdirected by people who do not live in the area and are committed to it only as professionals, not as citizens. The Government needs to work in partnership with faith-based groups to ensure that the best of the training, resourcing and support that can be provided by the state is given to non-partisan, non-ethnically-aligned services. There is no contradiction in a mosque receiving funding from the Government to run a debt-counselling service or a mentoring programme as long as it is available to everyone in the local community, whatever their religious or ethnic background—and that is the crucial point. The same holds true for a synagogue, a Sikh or Hindu temple or a church. If their congregations benefit from the scheme because people are drawn to their faith as a result of the contact they have had with it through using the service or programme, so much the better. A confident society should regard such funding as an investment.

## Restrict welfare to a limited period of time

One of the radical, controversial but ultimately successful policies that Bill Clinton introduced was to set a two-year limit on continuous welfare payments and a five-year limit on all payments over a mother's lifetime. The impact of this innovation has been to reduce the number of recipients of welfare and to encourage people to make the transition back from welfare to work.[60] Tough-love policies such as this may be needed to prevent people from becoming welfare junkies, passive and dependent on the state. It also encourages families to take more responsibility for their members rather than relying on the state to do so.

## Teach children to get involved in the community

Children develop many of their social values through education and this provides a vital context for them to be exposed to the needs of the vulnerable in the community. It is relatively simple to establish schemes in which schoolchildren get involved in visiting the elderly or the sick, helping to dig gardens or clear rubbish, repaint public buildings or work alongside single parents in playgroups.

## Reintroduce a period of National Service

National Service is just that: service to the nation, for the good of society. It need not be military. It can have a social function and focus, which is much more suitable to an age when military investment is diminishing, not growing. Given that the highest proportion of crimes are committed by young men between the ages of 18 and 25, this is the key stage when a period of national community service could have an enormous impact. Many young men do not feel they are part of any enterprise that involves self-discipline, but they need a strong, supportive structure around them and role models they can aspire to. A

---

[60] Frank Field, 'Less Carrot, More Stick', *The Daily Telegraph*, 6 March 2007. Retrieved on 6 April 2008 from http://www.telegraph.co.uk/opinion/main.jhtml?xml=/opinion/2007/03/06/do0602.xml

strong code of conduct, belonging to a group or team, learning to work under leadership as well as to take on leadership, developing the capacity to think of others and not just themselves—these are among the many potential benefits of a period of national service.

# SEVENTEEN

## Cohesion

# (PWC, Mass)

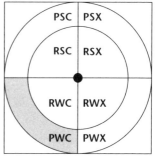

**Key Question: How do you foster social cohesion in an aspirational society?**

**Key Principle:**

*Many of our current aspirations (for health, fitness and well-being, to name just a few) can be met in more socially constructive ways than at present. Employers and local and national government can all adopt policies that help to encourage people to become more committed to their own communities.*

Human beings have a wonderful, powerful drive to improve their lot, and this needs to be harnessed rather than suppressed. Socialist forms of capital ownership have tended to deny this drive in individuals and, as a result, come unstuck. Some people will always seek to stand out from the crowd, and simply organizing people into crowds does not take away that impulse—those with an entrepreneurial streak simply find a way to work round the system to get ahead. Collectivist structures of ownership will always fail unless they also harness people's drive to improve their own circumstances. The trick is to promote the betterment of the individual and the betterment of society at the same time. It requires some imagination and innovation, but it is not impossible.

## *First exploit natural opportunities for self-improvement*

It is often observed that if only we chose to walk or cycle to work or dug our gardens and planted vegetables, rather than sitting in our cars or in front of our TVs, we wouldn't need to spend hours pounding treadmills and lifting weights in the gym. Our ecology very often contains within it the most natural and efficient ways for us to remain fit and healthy. It is only when we abuse that ecology that we have to devise artificial and expensive (and tedious) substitutes. The same, I suggest, holds true for our social health. If employers looked around them for the natural opportunities for enterprise partnerships with the local community and exercised their minds on those, they would find that the need for artificial social-training programmes, 'emotional intelligence' courses and the like would plummet. The most powerful learning (as practitioners of adult education are always saying) comes from our engagement with our environment. For the sake of economy and efficiency, if nothing else, we should be seizing such opportunities with both hands.

Here are some initiatives that corporations could start with:

- Encourage your employees to talk to someone on their journeys to and from work each day
- Encourage your employees to stop on their way to work and help someone who is in need, even if it might make them late at the office. This would involve teaching managers to see the value in members of their teams offering services outside the walls of the office. To be effective, it would require trust and responsibility from all concerned.
- Invite the staff of nearby stores into your offices to look around and see what went on behind your doors. This would make a connection between different sectors of business and the community and would cost almost nothing. In addition, during a festival you could even serve drinks.
- Hold some 'partners events' from time to time, where you invited your employees' partners to come for lunch or drinks after work to see what their other half got up to all week
- Second someone to sit on a local committee set up to improve the look of the street, the road layout or other local environmental concerns
- Hold an 'unusual transport day', when everyone was encouraged to find a different way to come into the office than the usual, just to see the world from a different angle
- Get your senior executives to accompany the cleaning staff or the amenities team around for half a day and help them in their work, so that they gained an understanding of the people who do the apparently less important jobs in the organization
- Begin every Friday in the office with a '10-minute think before you start' routine. From 8.30 to 8.40, say, the computers and PDAs would be turned off and phones set to silent. A room, or rooms, would be set aside where everyone could gather and just sit and think quietly—about the stress of the journey to work, about the day ahead—and acknowledge the 'stuff' they had brought into work that day. It would take some time

to make this part of your corporate culture, but it would dramatically change the way the day began.

· Make space on your premises for a garden, where your staff could grow some flowers and vegetables or fruit. I know the manager of a pig-iron-smelting works who planted a strawberry field on his site. His men loved to spend half an hour digging and hoeing instead of smelting iron. The same could be said for drafting corporate law contracts or doing company audits.

From such immediate, direct and local experience of social responsibility, I believe that deeper emotions and concerns would begin to flow. All of us tend to act on fairly basic emotional responses: for example, if I myself have recently been made redundant or bereaved, I am likely to feel far more compassion towards others who have suffered a similar loss than someone who doesn't know how it feels. Those who are most motivated to help others, and most active in caring for others, are often those who themselves have suffered and have also received care from others. A virtuous circle is created in which people in pain who choose to be compassionate then foster compassion in others. As someone has put it, a 'cascade of grace' begins to flow.

I believe we will see the same effect as we address the bigger problems that face our world, whether we are tackling global poverty, or seeking to change the economic system so that we value social capital as highly as financial capital and GDP, or trying to regulate supply chains and ensure fair wages. These challenges are too remote, too huge, too insurmountable for any one person, however well placed they may be, and their good intentions will come to nothing. However, if even one person is changed, even if the change is felt only locally, quite often it can precipitate something that will build into an ever-bigger 'cascade' of changes.

## Discourage hyper-mobility through taxation

As long as it is cheap for people to travel large distances to their work, to the shops, to their holiday destination, they will; but, as we now recognize, all our travelling is having a negative impact on both the built and the natural environment. Not only does it consume resources, it also distances us from each other, reducing our sense of cohesion. In dormitory towns, the daily commute has affected the life of the local community like a slow anaesthetic. However, people will work, shop and holiday more locally only when it is too expensive to do anything else. What we need is a radical approach to taxation on fuel and travel, which is quite practicable. For most of our societies it will be somewhat painful, but we are addicted to hyper-mobility and weaning anyone off an addiction usually hurts. Excessive travel is a luxury whose full costs could and should be paid for, and it will encourage most of us to work, rest and play closer to home. The incentives for people to invest once more in their local communities will grow.

# EIGHTEEN

## Conviction

## (RSX, Radical)

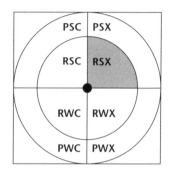

**Key Question: What is the role of faith in social well-being, and what are its dangers?**

**Key Principle:**

*Faith is an essential dimension of any healthy society. However, it gets corrupted when it becomes associated with any particular territorial expression. Faith will, and must, engage in dialogue with politics as a potent, prophetic and subversive voice, but it must not itself become politically manifest in a controlling system.*

At its most basic, being undefended is a matter of being able to trust yourself and others. Most defensive actions on the part of a state or society, whether military, political or economic, arise from a lack of trust. If I am able to trust both myself and you, I can believe the best of you rather than being suspicious of your agenda. I can find ways to share with you, in the belief that we may both benefit more from working together than from competing. I can offer you my culture, as well as receive yours.

This is a radical and idealistic vision for a nation. To be honest, it is only in fairy tales that nations actually do treat each other like that; and yet that should not stop us proposing the ideal or considering how our own nation could move towards it. Historically, we have seen grace, trust and freedom triumph more often in specific matters than in general throughout a culture. For example, in the abolition of the slave trade and then slavery we saw Europe and the Americas become less defended and more trusting and free, and the same goes for the ending of child labour, the regulation of working conditions, the establishment of the welfare state, the ending of segregation, the establishment of freedom of worship without risk of persecution and the enshrining in law of protection for unborn children. All of these developments represented advances into a less defended way of living together, in which threads of trust were woven into the social fabric.

Every generation needs the conviction that flows from shared ideals if it is to raise its eyes from its present situation towards something more noble. The ascent towards values that are more humane, more just, more liberated and more undefended requires an impulse to reach the top of the mountain. Often, that idealism has an explicitly spiritual dimension, which takes it out of the merely human, the merely material, into the transcendent. It is the spiritual that historically has proved to have the greatest capacity to inspire our noblest acts. However, many critics of its influence would argue that religion causes at least as many problems as it solves. Certainly it would be one-eyed to ignore all the ways in which faith and its social expression, religion, have led to more rather than less defendedness, and we need to reflect on why it is that religion fails to be a humanizing force and can actually become inhumane.

## *Territorial faith allied to political power is dangerous*

The problems associated with the impact of religious faith on human society have often arisen specifically when it has become allied with political power. The emperor Constantine in AD 312 embraced Christianity after seeing a vision in the sky before winning the battle of Milvian Bridge. His 'conversion' meant that Christianity became the official religion of the whole of the Roman Empire, and the persecution of Christians, who had once been thrown to the lions in the Colosseum, ceased. From that point on, the church in the West was hand-in-glove with the power of the state.

Although, looking back, we can see many ways in which Christianity had a civilizing influence on Roman rule, by the Middle Ages the church's grip on education, knowledge, authority and the laity's spiritual destiny was restrictive and oppressive. Moreover, in the 12th and 13th centuries it funded the Crusades that aimed to take back control of Jerusalem from the Muslims. The monasteries kept the keys of eternal life and death locked away in their scriptoria, where the monks copied the Bible out in Latin, as the church maintained its authority even over kings by preventing the laity from reading holy writ for themselves in their own language. The church's wealth grew as it sold spiritual favours and blessings through a system of penances and 'indulgences'. It was this systemic corruption and abuse of power that provoked the Reformation in the 16th century, under the leadership of the German theologian Martin Luther.

Luther insisted that the church should not control access to the scriptures, or to the remission of sins. The Reformers' cry 'By faith alone, through grace alone' expressed the conviction that salvation was available to everyone through a direct and personal act of faith in Jesus' death on the cross, rather than through the intercession of priests and through sundry acts of atonement performed by the church on the laity's behalf. The Reformation recognized that for many people the church had become a barrier preventing an encounter with God, and Luther argued that this 'good news' had always lain at the roots of the Christian message. Sadly, the reformed church failed to escape from its entanglement with institutional and state power—and indeed the English Reformation only consolidated its crucial role in the government of England and Wales.

The modern history of the church is tragically punctuated by the martyrdom of hundreds of so-called heretics, both Reformed and Roman Catholic, in waves of persecution. Like the Crusades, such shameful episodes arose out of a fundamentally mistaken alliance between the church and civil government. The Western church was infected with a territorialism that was entirely alien to its founder, Jesus: a territorialism that imposed a dogma, of creed, of uniform, of ethnicity, of culture and of education. Having come to identify itself with the physical territory of Europe, the church began to give its blessing to the defence of that territory by force. The religion it propagated provided the ideological basis for war and domination in the name of truth, justice and God. The Western church displayed a growing pattern of defendedness, rather than undefendedness. Its lack of trust led it to seek to control knowledge, power and money, and even the state, as well as to keep hold (as before) of the keys of eternal life and death. It also created a perspective that saw outsiders as threats rather than potential friends and justified both aggression and violent defence. Finally, it bred a culture of suspicion that insisted on top-down authority, which the Roman Catholic Church struggles to escape to this day.

If the story of the Christian church in the West is one of the entanglement of faith with political power and the territorialism that inevitably accompanies it, it is in this respect little different from that of some traditions of Islam, which is theologically susceptible to territorialism. Beginning with a doctrine of the universal rule of God, to which the *ummah* (the worldwide 'nation' of believers) must live in obedience, Muslims have at many points in history and in many places found they could only fulfil Islam by giving it physical and political expression. Many believe that the *ummah* cannot live rightly under God until they live in a theocracy, where God's law is enshrined in the laws of the state and everyone is required to submit to it. Like Orthodox Judaism, Islam considers that certain ground can be holy, which is why the issue of Jerusalem is so central to the various crises in the Middle East. Both Jews and Muslims claim its Temple Mount as holy in their own traditions, but more than that: many of them feel that it is defiled by the presence of the others. And since there is no practicable way to carve those few square metres of ground in two, the conflict may never finally be resolved.

When faith is territorial, or insists on being enshrined in the laws that govern the state, and as a result is allied with the structures and forces (including governments and armies) that rule human society, it becomes no more than another ideology whereby people can live lives defended from each other. Indeed, there is no one more defended than the religious zealot determined to stand on holy ground.

In Britain, the alliance between the Church of England and the state has been eroded and undermined systematically over the last century. Many in the church feel a great sense of bereavement as a result, seeing the demise of Christendom (created by Constantine 17 centuries ago) as a tragedy. Certainly the church has lost much of its power, but whether that is tragic is another matter. For some Christians, it presents an opportunity to establish a new and more appropriate relationship with the state, in which the power of God is understood non-politically.

Such a rift is less apparent in America. The rhetoric of the current 'war on terror' was initially religious, and even messianic, in tone, and it certainly seemed to be the case that George W Bush's neoconservative foreign policy was shaped by theology as well as politics. At a time when the Muslim world is all too ready to identify the West with Christendom and to see its political and economic domination as something to be opposed, Bush's language has merely heightened the antagonism, polarizing people and legitimizing territorial warfare on both sides. As is always the case when this happens, it is impossible to tease out how much of the resulting violence is informed by faith, how much by politics, how much by economics and how much by simple hatred, fear and desire for revenge.

## Does God take political sides?

As things stand, the territoriality of both these forms of Christianity and Islam is deeply problematic for the global population. There are those who argue that society is indeed best governed according to Christian principles, just as there are those who argue the same of shari'ah law. However, when you look in the Bible, the source of authority for the church throughout the ages, you find a distinct and striking ambivalence on the question of whether God can be identified with any human form of power. The fifth chapter of Joshua records an interesting encounter between the leader (and commander) of the Israelites and a man who is referred to as 'the commander of the Lord's army'. Joshua is on the brink of the land promised by God to his people; before him stands the defended city of Jericho (interestingly, a city that has been taken and retaken many times in its very long history). When he meets this angelic figure, 'standing in front of him with a drawn sword in his hand',[61] Joshua asks him whose side he is on, his or the enemy's. Given the story so far, in which God has led his people to this point so that they can take this land, you would expect him to align himself with the Israelites. However, he does not. 'Neither,' he replies, 'but as commander of the army of the Lord I have now come.'

This statement is deeply revealing. It highlights a truth found throughout the Bible: that God, even in his covenants with people, does not fight on one side or another in human battles. It seems he does not divide humankind along ethnic or national lines, as centuries later the apostle Paul made clear.[62] Instead, God assesses each individual according to the state of their heart.[63] He observes which of us seeks to live out our lives trusting him, and trusting in his servant Jesus, and which of us seeks to impose their own will and authority on their own life and others'.

Time and again, the Bible tells stories of people who would have been excluded on ethnic grounds but who are welcomed into God's grace and love, precisely to make this point: Rahab, the prostitute living in Jericho,[64] Naaman, the Syrian general,[65] Ruth the Midianite, the woman from Syrian Phoenicia,[66] the centurion in Capernaum[67]—each one disqualified by their race but included by grace. Indeed, the New Testament writer Matthew drew attention to the fact that Jesus, who he understood to be the Messiah, God's anointed, was descended not only from Jewish royalty but also from outsiders to the Jewish people, including Ruth.[68] He wanted us to grasp that Jesus himself represents God's merciful and generous hand reaching outside the territorial and ethnic limits of the people of Israel.

In fact, it is the message of scripture, abundantly clear throughout the Bible but made most explicit in the New Testament in the life and teachings of Jesus, that God's blessing is not conferred on ethnic, physical or geographical grounds. Rather, it is given to those who relinquish their own means to defend themselves and instead trust in the goodness of God to defend them. It is clear that God draws a single line through humankind, and it is not Bush's 'axis of evil': it's the line that divides those who are defended and those who are undefended, those who secure their own safety and those who trust God

---

[61] Joshua 5.13
[62] Galatians 3.28
[63] 1 Samuel 16.1–7
[64] Hebrews 11.31
[65] 2 Kings 5.1
[66] Mark 7.24–30
[67] Matthew 8.5–13
[68] Matthew 1.1–17

to make them safe, those who seek to justify themselves through their own worthiness and those who acknowledge their own corruption and depend entirely on the forgiveness available in Jesus Christ.

According to the Bible, God's hand is on the side of neither America nor al-Qa'ida. Those who say otherwise represent neither the freedom nor the undefendedness that are truly godly but, rather, the manifestations of defendedness and idolatry that have so distorted God's message that they have twisted it to meet their own ends of domination, fulfilment and control.

## *Is God undefended?*

In contrast to such ideologies, when we read the accounts of Jesus' life and teaching in the Bible we hear a voice that subverts the structures of power and authority in this world. In a well-known parable recorded in Matthew 22.1–14 and Luke 14.16–23, Jesus tells of a banquet laid on by a king for guests who are themselves rich and noble. However, each one finds an excuse not to attend. In frustration, the king instructs his servants to go out into the streets and alleys of the town, and even the country lanes, and bring in the poor, the crippled, the blind and the lame, 'both good and bad', to come and enjoy his banquet. Jesus tells this sharp and subversive parable to the Jewish rulers of his day in order to highlight the fact that God's invitation, though it does not exclude the powerful and the wealthy, is also extended to the weak and the poor. Not only so, but the latter are in fact more likely to accept it and be welcomed in, rather than the proud rich, who can think of better things to do.

Jesus tells many such stories to illustrate the fact that it's not that the powerful and the wealthy per se are barred from entering God's kingdom but that their power and wealth often make it very hard for them to be willing to do so. The reality is that for many of us our assets—be they assets of power, prestige, connections, riches or whatever—defend us: they enable us to feel in control, able to cope with whatever life throws at us. In contrast, God's kingdom is a place that is open to those who are willing to relinquish their defences and instead allow themselves to be defended by God alone (Matthew 5.1–9). In this way, they mirror the character of the King himself, who is himself undefended, who generously makes his world available for people to enjoy, who makes his love and forgiveness available through the death of his Son, Jesus, on a cross, who makes his life, potent enough to overcome death, available to those who will give up their own lives in service to him and his world (Mark 8.35).

Genuine spirituality is a spirituality of undefendedness, of generosity, which enjoys the resources we have but also freely gives them away. It lays down our 'territorial' claims to the ownership of our land, our money, our rights or even our lives. This is possible because ultimately we are secured by relationship with

God, which is strong enough to survive all of life's losses and privations, even death (Romans 8.38–39).

## The hunger for transcendence

The West desperately needs to find once again a source of spiritual life which can fund a more exalted vision of society. For too long the church has colluded with the state in a comfortable marriage, and as a result it has become assimilated into Western culture, almost indistinguishable from the wider society in its attitudes, ethics and message. It has ceased to be the provocative and prophetic voice it once was, speaking with conviction and compassion. Because until the middle of the last century it was allied with that society's historic structures of power, it has suffered the same fate as them: the influence of the church has declined along with those of the monarchy, institutional authority and political ideology. As George Santayana once observed, if you marry one generation, you are widowed in the next. It is for this reason that the church finds itself bereft of power and, almost, of title. Its language and its spirituality have little meaning for people today, and less appeal.

For its own sake and that of society, the church needs to find a new language in which to express its vibrant spirituality. Our society needs a distinctive spiritual voice to inform our moral narrative. There is nothing quite so depressing as a typical Sunday morning in Britain. By 11 a.m., out-of-town retail parks are filling up with shoppers who drift from garden centre to furniture store in a state of emotional numbness, their appetites dulled, robbed of anticipation yet drawn onwards, through sheer boredom, into the netherworld of shopping. This dystopian monoculture is a realization of the virtual world we are shown throughout the week via daytime satellite TV, where banks of shopping channels vie for a diminishing 0.01% market share.

My own experience is that many people in our society are crying out for an experience of transcendence. They have never known what it is to walk on holy ground, to enter a sacred space in which prayer has been offered for centuries and take off their shoes in the heavy silence of reverent awe. They have never been awakened to their own soul; they do not know what it is for that soul to touch the Other, to encounter what is beyond, what is older, deeper and more mysterious. They do not know the discipline of waiting, in stillness and denial of self, and paying attention to the Other. We are truly a generation of 'hollow men', superficial, thin, transparent, rootless, substanceless, weightless, in danger of being swept away by the slightest puff of wind. The church will be doing us all a fatal disservice if it offers us no more than another serving of spiritual retail therapy.

# NINETEEN

## Where Do We Go from Here?

London is without question the financial capital of Europe. Its two great financial centres are the City, the historic location of the Bank of England and the stock market, and Canary Wharf. They lie just three miles apart. The river Thames, that old artery of trade that made London the capital of England in the Dark Ages, snakes its way eastward, out to the North Sea. Passing St Paul's Cathedral, the City and Tower Bridge, it cuts its widening course towards the Isle of Dogs and the brilliant steel-and-glass towers of Canary Wharf. River taxis carrying suited businesspeople ply their way from City to Wharf, and the Docklands Light Railway whisks many another to their polished destinations, without ever touching the ground beneath them.

The land in between the City and Canary Wharf is a part of London once built on trade, when the Thames was deep enough for wooden ships laden with cargo to sail up that far. However, nowadays the redundant docks and basins of Shadwell and Wapping (their business having long gone east to the estuary mouth at Tilbury) are merely playgrounds for the wealthy, and expensive gated developments have sprung up along a narrow strip hugging the river. However, the wider landscape between the city's two centres of financial power is very different. Here, you will find what remains of the indigenous white working-class population. Shrunk to no more than a few thousand, mostly ageing folk, they have watched their livelihoods decay before their eyes. Ask them for their memories of the Blitz or the old London docks and they will tell you stories of almost pure regret: regret at the loss of their industry, regret at the intrusion of ethnic minorities, regret that their families have long since left for Epping, Basildon and Billericay (encouraged by Margaret Thatcher's sale of council houses in the Eighties), regret that the community clubs and the tea dances are things of the past.

This part of London has always been a first port of call for immigrants, from the Huguenots who moved into Whitechapel during the persecutions of the 17th century to the Jews, who established their sewing workshops, and now to the Bangladeshis. However, while once for such newcomers these streets were just the first rungs on the ladder to social status and prosperity elsewhere, the more recent arrivals seem to have become stuck there. The area is now

80-per-cent Bangladeshi and looks set to stay that way. Housed in large, run-down blocks in their own little world, hemmed in to the west and the east by the glittering towers and gleaming spires of the City and Canary Wharf, their situation is a living illustration of the planet's social ecology.

Within that five miles square you will see in miniature the global social landscape: the juxtaposition of two communities separated by a gulf in their ideology, opportunity and power. The City and Canary Wharf represent the interests of the domination of capital, the management of money that (as we have seen) has shaped the planet's social ecology. It represents the exercise of power through financial transactions which determine social and political reality. It exists now, on the very edge of its own cliff of aspiration, compelled by its own rules to seek to grow continually, relentlessly, unsupportably, to dominate and outdo all opposition. Thus, the physical geography of the area has come to reflect the psycho-geography of the planet: the sealed isolation of the West, working and travelling as if in a parallel world, fearful of intruders, trying to insulate itself from the influence, let alone the participation, of the rest of the global community. It justifies its existence with the arguments of capitalism, insisting that it will enrich the whole global system and that even a small slice of a bigger cake is better than a big slice of a small one. There is no trust and only inability to feel for another.

The reality is that unless London takes notice of this growing gulf, its own security and success will be jeopardized. How attractive a proposition for new investment will it be after a few more suicide attacks and a hundred more dead, with no prospect of containment? Global markets sail on confidence, and such waves of panic can swamp them instantly. The day for wilful negligence is surely over. We have to find an alternative—and that alternative must be rooted in the opposite commitments to those of fear and greed that sustain the current system. And the most important of these is trust.

## *Participation, not domination*

Trust entails the amicable sharing of resources. It chooses to believe the best of the other person and welcome them as a friend rather than suspect the worst and see them as a likely enemy. We might begin with the way we share this planet with other species. The Victorians recognized that nature was 'red in tooth and claw' and felt a sense of awe at the power of the biological world. With the afterglow of a creationist world view still imbuing the evolutionary theories of Darwin with light and hope, the natural world was a spectacle of incredible complexity and beauty. Rousseau's romantic vision of a primitive Arcadia saw human life connected indissolubly to the texture of the planet.

For the last century, however, we have set out not to admire our environment but to dominate it, severing ourselves from our biological roots and context as we strive to break the constraints of agricultural, genetic and ecological givens. Only now, in the early years of the 21st century, are we able to see that this project of the last hundred years was merely a brief (and unprecedented) transition between two ages, an interregnum in which we lived out a myth of our independence from the planet. Our technological 'mastery' of the biosphere will not deliver us from its fate, any more than the incantations of the Maya were able to stave off their demise.

Instead, we must accept once again that our future lies not in our domination over but in our participation in the natural world. We must trustfully share the resources we have been given to steward. We must entrust ourselves to the world around us, aware that finally we cannot subdue and control nature but instead must accept a providential relationship of mutual trust and respect. And this relationship must, and can only, begin with humankind. How can we respect the environment if we cannot respect each other? Living trustfully in relation to the natural world will be possible only if we begin to live trustfully with one another. And in the end our ability to take this path depends on our willingness to respect not just our environment, not just other people but our very selves. Choosing to respect our own dignity as marvellous, mysterious but dependent and fragile creatures will lead to us to treat others, and our world, in the same way.

## *Personal initiatives*

Once, *The Times* invited a number of eminent authors to write an essay on the theme 'What is wrong with the world?' G K Chesterton sent in his contribution in the form of a letter. It read:

> Dear Sirs,
> I am.
> Sincerely yours,
> G K Chesterton

His response provides us with a crucial insight into the human condition. The root of our problems in society, whether nationally or globally, lies not in society itself but in the individuals who make up society. This book has focused intentionally on the social mechanisms that constrain and shape the behaviour of human populations and has sought to understand the nature of the social problems facing us all. As such, it has addressed the systemic problems more than the problems of the individual within the system. However, it is the third of a trilogy of books, the first two of which set out the responsibility the individual has within the system. Although it is vital to understand the patterns of the whole, I cannot personally escape an evaluation of my own life. Indeed, it is my own life over which I have some degree of control, and so expediency if nothing else dictates that this is where I should focus my attention.

Let me be honest: I have not enjoyed writing this book. I do not like the implications that its arguments and conclusions have for me and my lifestyle. I am anxious about the hypocrisies in my own life. I feel concerned and guilty about the footprints I have left—and continue to leave—on the planet. I am sceptical about my own willingness and ability to live a more responsible and less defended life. I am fully aware that I am a part of the system I am critiquing, and that I use its machinery to promote my own ends and perspectives. I need also to be honest that I do not know all the answers. I do not see an easy or clear set of choices in terms of how we should buy our goods, travel to our work, pursue our interests or raise our children. I find there are more questions than answers.

## *Idealism* and *pragmatism*

I am torn between idealism and pragmatism. The idealist inside me points to a distant yet beautiful horizon where the human race experiences a deep and genuine inner reformation and a renewal of its cultural, moral and spiritual life. The pragmatist whispers that such ideals lead only to disappointment and disillusion, that politics is a matter of compromise and accommodation, that you must trim your sails and tack slowly and realistically into the wind towards some more achievable, modest and ultimately acceptable goals. However, I have come to see that idealism and pragmatism are not incompatible and that perhaps we must seek to hold the two together, the one speaking to our hearts, our souls and our imaginations, the other to our minds and hands. We are, after all, human beings with all of these components. I am content, then, that I must create within myself room for the idealist and the pragmatist to sit together and converse with each other. A lively and creative, if at times unsettling, dialogue must be sustained. I hope this book can achieve a similar balance of idealism and pragmatism: enough of one to allow us to contemplate the better horizons that humankind must aim for, enough of the other to ensure we are not disregarded and to offer us some reasonable steps that every one of us can take.

In the spirit of this tension, which I accept I cannot resolve (and perhaps if I were able to, my energy and passion would dissipate anyway), I intend to cultivate both my idealism and my pragmatism. I intend to sustain, and deepen, the spiritual intensity and vision for life that fund my idealism. At the same time, I commit myself to active, realistic, engaged participation in the problems of the world as we encounter them, seeking whatever ad hoc solutions we can find.

I appeal to you to do the same. On the one hand, I want to encourage you to consider practical ways in which you can start to make a difference to your own world. There are all kinds of changes you can make this very day. Here are a few suggestion, which I offer just to stimulate your own thinking…

## What we consume

Let's start with the way we travel. Are there ways we can cut down on our use of our cars? Could we walk or cycle, use public transport or share a lift? Some of us can save money by cycling to work (not least by cancelling our subscription to the gym, as we'll no longer need it). Some of us might be able to get a car-sharing scheme going at work. And then there is the issue of air travel…

Then we might consider our use of energy. Simply changing light bulbs to low-energy types, turning equipment off rather than leaving it on standby, washing the dishes by hand rather than using the dishwasher, hanging your laundry out to dry rather than using the tumble drier—these simple changes to your lifestyle will reduce your consumption of electricity, and water, dramatically. Then there is the option of renewable energy: switch to a renewable-power supplier, or find out whether you can harness wind or solar (or even geothermal) power yourself at home. Many people have cut their energy bills almost to zero by such means. Consider wearing a lovely, warm sweater indoors in the winter, rather than turning up the central heating so you can live at 25°C all year round. Consider sharing the bathwater with someone else in the family, or taking a shower instead.

Then, consider what you buy. Reuse the plastic bags the supermarket gives you, or take your own. Buy vegetables loose rather than washed and packaged. Put pressure on the supermarkets to stock more goods loose, or find out whether you can buy more local produce from a farm. Consider pick-your-own, which children usually enjoy (they get to stuff their faces with strawberries or blackberries, and also learn where food comes from). Of course, that would mean buying fruit when it's in season, which means you can't have apples and berries all year round—but then when they come, you'll appreciate them twice as much! It's a simple and practicable bit of self-discipline that will reward us with greater pleasure.

## Where we work

How about your place of work? You may be able to assemble a working party to consider how your office or school can reduce its consumption of both energy and material resources. You might consider if you could switch to renewable energy, recycled paper, low-energy light bulbs. Simple education can also help to create a culture of awareness and sensitivity to our impact on the environment: turning of the lights when leaving a room, shutting down the computer instead of leaving it on standby, putting only as much water in the kettle as you need, driving to your meeting with the windows down rather than using the air-con.

## Where we live

As well as reducing our consumption (and saving money as well as resources in the process), there are immediate ways we can choose to improve our human ecology as well as our environment. As an exercise, think about your immediate neighbourhood for a moment, wherever you happen to live. Imagine that the people in that place are connected by a network of invisible threads, which represent the social bonds between them. Think about the people who are joined by the thinnest, weakest and perhaps fewest threads. It might be the elderly people who rarely go out, it might be the young family on benefits, isolated and carless, it might be the teenage boys who live in their own world of gaming and texting, it might be the immigrant family who have different clothes and a different rhythm of life, it might be the disabled woman or the young man suffering from a mental disorder who is very difficult to talk to. Each of us lives in a neighbourhood where someone (at least) is in danger of becoming detached altogether from the social fabric. Think about what you could do to strengthen the connections between them and the community. It might begin with little more than an intentional conversation next time you pass them on the street.

- Maybe you have a garden and can invite a few people round for lemonade and biscuits.
- If you have a Christmas party, maybe you could invite all your neighbours rather than just your friends.
- Maybe you could pop into the local old people's home and offer to visit, with your children, once a fortnight; or maybe you could volunteer to work at the local homeless shelter.
- Maybe you and your children could do up a garden once a year.
- Maybe you could find out whether there is a local scheme you could volunteer for to mentor a teenager.

Some of these ideas are simple and personal; others, which concern our work or communities, may be more structural and formal. Both kinds are needed and neither kind needs to be very costly.

## Sponsoring someone else

One of the most enjoyable ways to connect with issues further away from home is to sponsor a child or a community in a majority-world country. Organizations exist that run well-executed and effective schemes, with projects that reliably deliver education, finance and support. There is nothing more rewarding than corresponding with your 'adopted' child in Bolivia or India, and building that relationship over the years. I know people who have 'adopted' dozens of children in this way. And your kids, if you have any, will love to do so, too. They may also enjoy buying their grandma a nanny goat for Christmas—only, the goat will be given to a family in Mozambique rather than standing in grandma's backyard! This kind of scheme, which is rapidly growing in popularity, is a fun way to celebrate Christmas while recognizing that often there is really nothing we are lacking ourselves.

## How we invest

If you want to go one stage further, consider ethical investment. In this case, the vehicle you invest in supports a set of ethical values and aspirations as well as financial ones. There are plenty of ethical funds setting up in which money is invested in community schemes, social enterprises or just industries that are looking to benefit people and not harm them. The attraction is that your money grows at the same time as the causes you want to support. Why support causes you don't believe in?

Perhaps the most exciting kind of investment there is at the moment is microfinance. This involves a range of financial services available on micro levels to local communities in the majority world who don't have access to conventional banking. The most important of these services, perhaps, are capital investment loans, which often amount to less than $50 per client borrower! A tiny loan like that can be all that a woman in Sierra Leone needs to buy a sewing machine and set up a business that can in time earn enough to not only feed her family but also send her children to school.

'Microloans' are administered through local 'trust banks', which are essentially collectives of 20 or so client borrowers in the neighbourhood who agree to give security for each other's loans.

The members of the trust bank, all of whom receive loans to run their businesses, ensure that none of them default on their loan repayments, as otherwise the whole group will have to carry the can. In this way, the bank empowers its clients (very often all women), builds social cohesion and achieves remarkable rates of repayment (over 99 per cent). Thus, the donated funds can be recycled many times, which makes the system far more efficient and productive than aid-based projects.[69]

Many Westerners are sceptical about giving money to the majority world, aware that often it simply disappears in bureaucracy, mismanagement, waste or corruption. Microfinance doesn't offer aid; it fosters trade. It gives people a leg-up rather than a handout and sets in motion a virtuous circle of trust, empowerment and opportunity.

It costs a mere $8,000 to set up an entire trust bank and transform a community.

I know of several schools in the affluent suburbs of Oxford that have raised the money to do just that, several times over, and now have vibrant, robust, continuing relationships with village communities in Ghana.

Investing our financial capital so as to generate social capital is an example of undefended leadership.

### Where we worship

Faith communities at their best provide examples of authentic undefended relationships, as well as being catalysts and engines for all kinds of mission or outreach that demonstrates compassion and creativity both locally and globally. For many people, the confidence and conviction to give themselves in such a way can only have a spiritual source. I know it is indispensable for me.

## *Living the undefended life*

On the one hand, then, I want to be pragmatic: to take small, immediate, achievable steps to make some kind of difference. They may not change the world in one go, but they are at least heading in the right direction. On the other hand, I want to hold on to my deeper aspiration to live a more radical, undefended life. This is an ideal that demands that I see others not as hostile strangers but as potential friends, that my thoughts and actions are not concerned with my own advantage but authentically and freely address the needs of others. In the undefended life, another person is regarded not as a threat to be dealt with, a rival to be beaten or a commodity to be exploited but as someone with whom you should share yourself in trust. Moreover, you see yourself not as an agent that needs to be defended from danger but instead as a potential gift to others.

---

[69] For further information, see the UNCDF's *Microfinance Matters*, issue 17 (October 2005), found on 6 April 2008 at http://www.uncdf.org/english/microfinance/pubs/newsletter/pages/2005_10/Microfinance_Matters_Issue_17.pdf.

To live an undefended life does not at all mean being a doormat for others to trample over. Being undefended is not incompatible with (at times) being strong, assertive, authoritative, even dominant. I have set out as clearly as I can in the first two books in this trilogy, *Leading out of Who You Are* and *Leading with Nothing to Lose*, the levers of power and structures of authority that are available appropriately to the undefended leader. It is an act of undefended love to reach out and grab a child who has stepped out in front of an oncoming car and yank them with all your might back to safety. Indeed, to be passive in that moment would be a demonstration of heartlessness that had nothing to do with the kind of life I am advocating. It is undefended concern that ensures that we have laws that protect the vulnerable from those who would otherwise try to exploit or hurt them.

An undefended life is one in which you set aside your own personal interests for the sake of others. There are a few well-known examples in recent history that can inspire us today. Mother Teresa of Calcutta is one, who opened her heart to the plight of the 'untouchables' and lived among them. Mahatma Gandhi is another, who was willing to embrace sacrifice and suffering in order to identify himself with the people of India and empower them. Jimmy Carter is another, who as president of America pursued generous and humanitarian policies at a cost to his own reputation, and then went on not to do something glamorous and lucrative and high-profile but to build houses for the homeless with his own hands. Gordon Wilson, whose daughter, Marie, was killed by the IRA in the Enniskillen bombing, said he '[bore] no ill will … no grudge' towards her murderers and would pray for them 'tonight and every night'. He is another. Maximilian Kolbe, the Polish priest in Auschwitz who volunteered to be starved to death instead of another man who had a wife and children, is another.

Countless others have suffered similarly as they confronted the evil in the world—Dietrich Bonhoeffer, resisting Nazism, Martin Luther King, resisting racism, thousands of others resisting oppression all over the world. Countless more have at some point in their lives made undefended choices, often unrecognized. When Bill Gates made a commitment to give away most of his billions before he dies, that to me was an undefended act. The example of such people presents a noble alternative to the celebrities who parade before us, and we would do well to fix our eyes on their virtues. Few of us will be called to such heroism, and fewer still to martyrdom (though, of course, some may); but what we see in such women and men is that they did not love life so much that they shrank from death. For them, life had such deep roots that it could not be cut off by mere physical death.

In the West, we have long lacked such convictions, and their confidence seems to us extreme and perhaps unsettling. In recent years, we have understood a willingness to sacrifice your life only in the case of the destructive and immoral work of the suicide bomber who chants: 'You love life, we love death.' Suicide that embraces death as a justified and noble way to execute warfare and destruction of the enemy must not be confused with the generous sacrifice of your life to preserve the lives of others. A man such as Father Kolbe did not trade his life for the broken bodies and severed limbs of children, men and women, destroyed in the name of victory and domination.

The undefended life may be full, fulfilled, creative, long and productive as well as difficult, opposed and misunderstood. Ultimately, it involves relinquishing control over your own powers and assets and holding them lightly. It is about seeing ownership—of our money, our time, our skills, our power—in a different way. Instead of viewing these things as possessions to exploit to our profit, we choose to regard them as things entrusted to us for the benefit of others. They are gifts to humankind, not us alone. We are their stewards, not their owners.

We are free to accept and enjoy wealth, but we are also at liberty to let it go and give it away. We are not the slaves of our status or power, but are free from them. Not that we regard these things as dangerous or wrong in themselves— such asceticism is itself not free—but instead we receive with open hands and give with open hands. The richest man in the world, as well as the poorest, may be undefended—though if they were to meet, the encounter might alter their relative wealth!

It's important to emphasize that an undefended life is not necessarily one that is financially poor: it does not involve always denying yourself and missing out on the pleasures of life. That is asceticism, which is something else altogether. The undefended person is free to enjoy and receive the good things around her, as well as to give them up. Ultimately, she does not see herself as an environmental crusader, who ends up condemning enjoyment in order to save the planet. Rather, her goal is to live out an undefended life in the confidence that, if the whole of humankind did the same, we would find ourselves receiving and enjoying the goodness and generosity of the world in a sustainable way.

Worship—which is what I believe I am created to offer—is a matter of living a fully human, undefended life, receiving God's resources, rather than justifying my own pious existence through self-discipline and self-denial. As Irenaeus wrote, 'Gloria Dei vivens homo' (which is usually glossed as 'The glory of God is a human being fully alive').[70]

Ultimately, I believe that our goal is not to be frugal, ascetic or poor: it is to be free, and undefended in that freedom. Free to receive and enjoy, free to give away and lose ourselves. Such undefendedness can be ours only if we do not need our assets to secure us. I am able to receive as well as to let things go only

---

[70] Irenaeus, *Against the Heresies*, 4.20

if my deepest needs for identity, meaning, affection, belonging and intimacy are already provided for.

You may not agree, but it is my conviction that we inhabit a generous universe, made so by the liberality of the One who created it and continues to sustain it. We encounter that generosity in our lives through the food we eat, the love and approval we receive, the opportunities we enjoy and so on. All 'good' things we experience are gifts to us, expressions of God's care. They are also invitations to us to live like children who trust the providence of a divine Father, rather than fearfully storing up goods to ensure that we have enough. As we learn to receive such gifts with open hands, we begin to find that the world becomes a more generous place.

The person we live next to becomes a true neighbour, who we can choose to bless every day in simple ways, with a greeting, a warm smile, an offer of help, a willingness to listen rather than rush on.

- The elderly person living opposite ceases to be a 'crabby old nuisance' peering from behind his net curtains and instead becomes a friend who has much to give us—reminiscences, insights, even regrets—as well as reminding us of what we ourselves are going to become.
- The glass of orange juice in the morning is no longer a gulp before we run out of the door but a simple delight, first anticipated and then savoured.
- The flight on the plane is transformed from a tedious and exhausting haul to a wonderful opportunity—and, indeed, a privilege future generations may not have—to travel above the clouds and see the curve of the Earth from the edge of space.
- The world around us is teeming with life, generous life, from which we benefit and in which we participate. We have so much—and yet, so often, we appreciate so little. Again, the myth of desire robs us of enjoyment, making us unsatisfied with what we already have, persuading us that we must acquire more. Not so! We must acquire less and enjoy more—and as we do so we will find that there is plenty to go around, that we do not go short when we are generous to a stranger. We will begin to receive life rather than grabbing it. We will find that grace replaces whatever we give away.

This may be a fantasy, but even if it is, it's an intriguing one, isn't it? If only for the sake of the adventure, and the slightest chance that it may be true, perhaps it is worth giving it a go. Why not? What is stopping us from making a change, trying out something different for a week? It would be something to put in the Christmas letter, at any rate… What a shame it would be to die without trying something that, if it were true, would revolutionize your life—and not just your life but the lives of many others, too. What is stopping you? It may just be worth a whirl. And if you have come this far in the story, maybe you are willing to go just this little bit further...

## *The rule of life*

Many faith traditions have recognized the value of a clear set of stated principles for life. Sometimes these are referred to as a code, or a discipline, or a pattern, or a rule. One of the best-known Christian rules is that of Benedict, who recognized the need for human beings to live stable, committed, earthy lives.

The danger of any such rule is that it becomes a set of rules—and we all know what rules are used for: as pretexts to punish us when we break them. If we think of a rule of life like that, it will quickly become oppressive and counterproductive.

The Latin word from which we get 'rule' is regula, which can also mean a straight line or a benchmark. This might suggest that a rule of life is simply a way of drawing a straight line for us to aim at. I tend to think of myself as a climbing plant, whose stem lacks the strength to grow in a straight line unless it is tied to a frame of some kind. A rule of life is like such a frame: it helps me to observe and adjust how I am living and it keeps me aiming in the right direction.

Those who take part in my course on undefended leadership are invited to use a rule of life that encapsulates the principles both of the course and of this trilogy of books. It is structured around three values: receiving, welcoming and stewarding. I include it here in the hope that it may be of benefit to any reader who wants to live an undefended life themself.

### Receiving

Our attitude to the world is primarily that of receiving the goodness and generosity of the created order (and therefore the Creator). This is in contrast to a posture of 'giving to' or 'taking from', which implies the priority of our initiative, power and action. As those who receive, we accept our contingency and our codependence on the world, on our fellow humans and on the Creator. We also presuppose that the world, as created, is essentially a generous gift to be received with gratitude.

### Welcoming

Our commitment is to see others around us as friends whom we choose to welcome rather than as threats we have to avoid or protect ourselves from. Moreover, they are friends on the basis not of their behaviour, or their attractiveness to us, but of their shared createdness. Welcoming others involves a choice basically to trust them, and it implies vulnerability: making ourselves open to others in conversation, sharing our time or resources. Being welcoming is not, however, indiscriminate: it implies responsibility. Closing the door on someone else may be necessary and right when it is done to protect the vulnerable and to help the other to take responsibility for their actions.

## Stewarding

We understand that the world we have been given is finite and so are its resources. We also understand that those resources, of energy, food, space and raw materials, are being consumed recklessly, unfairly and unsustainably. We also understand that when we consume resources unsustainably we are stealing, not only from people living elsewhere on this planet but also from our children and our children's children. The obligation on us all is to 'tread lightly' on our environment—whether emotional, social, biological or physical—and to be deeply aware of the footprint we are leaving on the surface of our world.

| Value 1: Receiving | Value 2: Welcoming | Value 3: Stewarding |
|---|---|---|
| ...a daily rhythm of receiving at the start of the day before giving or taking, through simple, personal acts of prayer, contemplation, meditation or praise | ...cultivating the patience and stillness to listen attentively to those we meet so that each person feels heard and not ignored, used or passed over | ...choosing to engage in creative activity—social enterprise, creative or intellectual innovation or experimentation, and so on—so that our overall impact is positive, not negative |
| ...a practice of pausing before eating a meal in thanksgiving for the gift to be received | ...resisting the temptation to condemn others who hold different beliefs, and choosing instead to listen and understand their perspective and concerns in order to find ways to live as friends | ...adding to the social capital of our neighbourhood by visiting the vulnerable |
| ...a weekly discipline of setting aside time, at the start of the new week, to look ahead and receive its tasks, pleasures and encounters as opportunities for growth | ...communicating our beliefs, or those of our community, clearly and authentically so that others can see how they can relate to us, understand us and accept us | ...strengthening bonds in our family by being a peacemaker |
| ...a practice of cultivating an awareness of each season of nature, or 'season' of life, and adjusting what we eat, do and how we work accordingly | ...developing a commitment to help others to understand the impact of their actions and beliefs both on those around them and themselves, so that they can better take responsibility | ...deepening the relationships we have committed ourselves to so they with integrity and generosity |

| Value 1: Receiving | Value 2: Welcoming | Value 3: Stewarding |
|---|---|---|
| …an annual discipline of beginning each new year with a day (or more) of retreat | …choosing to view encounters with strangers as meetings with potential friends—a gift rather than a burden | …working to protect social structures and institutions that increase social capital and trust and opposing that which subverts them |
| …an attitude of thankfulness throughout the day for the things in life we take for granted (rain, fruit juice for breakfast, a warm bed, a job, income, family and so on) | …choosing to be especially attentive, in the use of our time, skill and money, to the vulnerable, the dispossessed, the homeless and the lost | …cultivating our own skills as gifts entrusted to us for the good of others, so that we can make the best contribution we can to the world |
| …a freedom to enjoy without guilt the delights, riches and goods of the world that come to us | …choosing to welcome visitors generously, whether they are expected or not, being willing to share with them as far as possible our home, our time and our food so that we may bless them as we have been blessed | …choosing to limit our consumption of the world's resources—energy, food, water, raw materials and so on—according to what we need, by being careful, efficient and restrained |
| …a conscious check on our impatience, frustration and even rage when circumstances appear to conspire against us | …choosing to offer back a proportion of our time and/ or money as a gift, to be given away freely with no thought of a return, as an act of dependence, trust and generosity and a sign that we are not mastered by greed | …considering the impact on the environment of our means of transport |
| …a decision to try to seek the learning and growth that may lie within the difficulties and afflictions that from time to time we have to endure | …developing a practice of confessing to those we may have hurt and asking for and receiving their forgiveness | …choosing to reduce the impact of our consumption on the planet by reducing waste (including packaging) and, as far as possible, repairing rather than replacing (including white goods, electronics, cars and so on) |
| …a pattern of periodic planned fasting (from such things as television, food, alcohol etc) as a way to master our desires | …seeking to surrender our anger over what has been wrongly done to us, rather than allowing it to fester and turn into bitterness, and in this way to find the resources to forgive those who hurt us | …choosing to consider the origins of all we consume, the conditions of those who produced it and the impact of the processes and materials used in its production (which may involve switching to a renewable-power supplier, for example, or buying local produce) |

# Select Bibliography

Charles Darwin. *On the Origin of Species: By Means of Natural Selection or The Preservation of Favoured Races in the Struggle for Life*. London: J Murray, 1859

Emile Durkheim. *Suicide: A Study in Sociology*. Translated by J A Spaulding and G Simpson. London: Routledge & Kegan Paul, 1952

T S Eliot. 'Choruses from The Rock', in *Collected Poems 1909–1962*. Faber and Faber, 1963

David Harvey. *The Condition of Postmodernity: An Enquiry into the Origins of Cultural Change*. Cambridge, MA: Blackwell, 1990

Irenaeus. *Irenaeus Against Heresies: Book 4*. Whitefish, Mont: Kessinger Publishing, 2007

Oliver James. *Britain on the Couch: Why We're Unhappier Compared with 1950 Despite Being Richer: a Treatment for the Low-Serotonin Society*. London: Century, 1997

J Richard Middleton and Brian J Walsh. *Truth Is Stranger than It Used To Be: Biblical Faith in a Postmodern Age*. London: SPCK, 1995

John Perkins. *Confessions of an Economic Hit Man*. San Francisco: Berrett-Koehler Publishers, 2004

Sayyid Qutb. *Milestones*. Beirut: The Holy Koran Publishing House, 1980

Robert A Rosenbaum and Doublas Brinkley. *The Penguin Encyclopedia of American History*. New York: Penguin Reference, 2003

# The Leadership Community

Simon Walker's The Undefended Leader trilogy developed out of his work with a number of leaders in business, charity, politics or the church who make up an on-line community, The Leadership Community. The Community is an ongoing association which is supported by a website (www.theleadershipcommunity. org). It provides many resources for those who want to offer undefended leadership, including training courses, conferences, web tools and on-line discussion forums. You can become a free guest member of the community through a simple online registration process.

The Leadership Community is committed to practice: we are members because we are trying to live out a certain kind of life. The only condition of membership is that you choose to join us.

**www.theleadershipcommunity.org**

# The Undefended Leader trilogy
## *by Simon Walker*

### LEADING OUT OF WHO YOU ARE

Discovering the Secret of Undefended
Leadership

ISBN: 978 1903689 43 1

### LEADING WITH NOTHING TO LOSE

Training in the Exercise of Power

ISBN: 978 1 903689 44 8

### LEADING WITH EVERYTHING TO GIVE

Lessons from the Success and Failure of Western
Capitalism

ISBN: 978 1903689 45 5

*"Leadership is commonly associated with dominance and
power. Simon Walker shows that there are other types of
leadership capable of being more effective."*
R Meredith Belbin

www.piquanteditions.com